BENEATH THE KILLING FIELDS

A Family Remembers

PETER CHHIM

Design: Roberta Morris, Leave It to 'Berta

First Edition: September 2025

ISBN Paperback: 979-8-9931147-0-5

ISBN eBook: 979-8-9931147-1-2

This is a work of nonfiction. All stories are based on real events, people, and interviews. Names, dates, and details are presented as accurately as possible based on family accounts and survivor testimony.

Printed in the United States of America

For my family—
whose memories, scars, and strength made this book possible.
And for the survivors of the Khmer Rouge,
and the generations who carry their stories forward.

From left: Ratana Chhim, Chhan/John Chhim,
Panha/Peter Chhim, Sokonni/Lori Chhim, Sorth Chhim,
Ratha Chhim, Vichinyi Chhim, Sitha Mean/family friend,
date 1979, refugee camp

Historical Primer: Who Were the Khmer Rouge?

"To keep you is no benefit. To destroy you is no loss."
— *Khmer Rouge slogan*

IN THE SPRING OF 1975, the Cambodian capital of Phnom Penh fell silent. The Khmer Rouge, a radical communist movement led by Pol Pot, had seized power after a years-long civil war. Victorious soldiers, dressed in black pajamas and sandals made from tires, flooded the city. At first, many Cambodians welcomed the end of fighting. They didn't yet understand that what followed would become one of the most brutal genocides of the twentieth century.

The Khmer Rouge believed they could transform Cambodia into a pure, classless society—free from capitalism, religion, modernity, and foreign influence. To achieve that vision, they began by emptying every city within days of taking power. Millions of Cambodians were forced at gunpoint to leave their homes, hospitals, and schools with only what they could carry. Children and the elderly alike were marched into the countryside under a blazing sun, many dying along the way.

Families were systematically separated—husbands from wives, children from parents—so that the individual's loyalty would belong to the revolution alone. People were assigned to harsh labor camps where they dug canals, grew rice, and built infrastructure by hand, often for twelve to fourteen hours a day without sufficient food or rest. Any sign of resistance, nostalgia, affection, or religious belief was dangerous. Even asking questions could mean death.

Education was abolished. Money was eliminated. Markets were shut down. Schools were turned into torture centers. Buddhist monks, artists, and intellectuals were among the first to be executed. People with glasses or soft hands—seen as evidence of education or privilege —were often singled out and killed.

Children were recruited into surveillance squads and taught to report their own families. The Khmer Rouge declared that Year Zero had begun. Cambodia's long history was erased overnight.

In less than four years, an estimated 1.7 to 2 million people died— from starvation, disease, overwork, or execution. That's nearly one in every four Cambodians.

The regime collapsed in 1979 after neighboring Vietnam invaded and drove the Khmer Rouge from power. But by then, Cambodia was devastated. Entire communities were wiped out. Rice fields were filled with mass graves—later known as the Killing Fields.

In the aftermath, survivors poured into refugee camps along the Thai border. Families were broken, malnourished, and traumatized. Some would live in those camps for years before being resettled in countries like Canada, the United States, France, or Australia. Others returned to what remained of their homeland, trying to rebuild amid ruins.

The full impact of the Khmer Rouge is not just in the number of lives lost—it is in the silence that followed. Many survivors did not speak of what happened, even to their children. The trauma was too deep. The pain too fresh. And the world, for the most part, looked away.

Introduction -The Silence We Inherited

BEFORE I EVER ASKED A QUESTION, I sensed there was something we weren't supposed to talk about.

My earliest memories in Canada are ordinary—plastic chairs in school cafeterias, snowy sidewalks, the static hum of TV sets in the evening. But in the background of that suburban childhood was a kind of emotional gravity, something heavy and invisible. My parents smiled often, but behind their smiles was a tiredness I couldn't name. My siblings laughed, but they also flinched at certain smells, certain songs, or the sound of distant shouting. There was love in our house—but also quiet.

Not the peaceful kind. The kind that carried weight.

As I got older, I began to realize this silence wasn't unique to my family. It was something I saw in the eyes of other Cambodians in our community—people who had started new lives in Canada, Australia, France, the US, and beyond. They spoke of hard work, of the future, of getting ahead. But rarely—almost never—did they speak of before. Not before Canada, not before the refugee camps, and certainly not before the war. The past, it seemed, had been buried, and what remained were fragments: stories half-told, names unspoken, a country reduced to shadows in grainy color and black-and-white photographs.

I was born in December 1977, near the end of the Khmer Rouge genocide. My birth was not a joyous celebration—it was an act of quiet defiance. I arrived into a world my family was desperate to escape. Two years later, we fled to a refugee camp in Thailand. I was a toddler. I don't remember the smell of the camp or the feel of dust on the floor where we slept. But I know it shaped us. And when we came to Canada in 1981—sponsored by a Catholic church group—I was only three. My memories of the war are not my own. But I carry them just the same.

For a long time, I didn't know how to carry them. I didn't know how to ask. And even if I had, I don't know if anyone would have answered.

But eventually, I started listening.

This book began not with a clear idea, but with a feeling—a tug, a need to understand. I had grown up hearing scraps of information: that my father escaped by boat; that my sister worked in mobile labor camps; that my brother had been punished in front of others. But no one sat me down to tell me these things. They emerged in fragments— during family dinners, whispered arguments, or when one of my older siblings accidentally dropped their emotional guard.

I started to write because I was afraid of forgetting.

And what I found when I began talking—really talking, for the first time—to my parents and siblings was staggering. These weren't just family stories. These were histories. These were testimonies. These were lives lived on the razor's edge of death and survival. Stories of endurance, betrayal, loyalty, and trauma. Stories that had been buried because remembering was too painful. But once the dam broke, the stories flowed. Often tearfully. Sometimes angrily. Always with purpose.

Each one had its own voice.

Each one carried the weight of a lost world.

Cambodia, for many of us, is both homeland and haunted land. The name itself evokes contradiction: a place of lush rice fields and geno- cide; of sacred temples and unspeakable horror. The beauty of our culture has always existed alongside the brutality of its history. And for those of us born into exile—those who only know Cambodia through stories, food, and inherited grief—our understanding is tangled.

We were not there, and yet we are shaped by what happened there.

This book, *Beneath the Killing Fields*, is my attempt to bridge that space.

When people hear about Cambodia, they often start with the numbers: nearly 2 million murdered by the Khmer Rouge between 1975 and 1979, nearly a quarter of the population. That's the fact most headlines carry.

It's difficult to fathom this kind of horror.

And when history feels too vast, we tend to retreat into generalizations. We say "genocide" and forget the people who died had names. We say "refugee" and forget what it means to walk across a minefield carrying your child. We say "survivor" but don't ask what they had to survive after the war—grief, guilt, silence, alienation, the unbearable task of rebuilding.

This book refuses to let those people be statistics.

It gives them voices. Real ones. And not all of them are perfect or heroic. Some of them are still processing. Some still carry anger. Some are only now beginning to grieve what they lost. But in every voice, there is dignity. In every story, truth.

This book is a collection of stories from one family that lived through it all. It is not a history textbook. I am not a historian. This book is memory—preserved, rediscovered, and passed on. I am the son of survivors. I grew up in Canada—a child of Cambodian refugees—trying to make sense of two worlds. At school, I recited the national anthem and played soccer on icy fields. At home, I watched my parents light incense at a family altar and speak of "home" like it was both distant and sacred. I often felt caught between those identities—not Canadian enough, not Cambodian enough. Writing this book became a way to reconcile that.

Each chapter is based on personal interviews with my family. Some were recorded formally. Others unfolded slowly over years of conversation. The people you'll meet in these pages are my siblings, my parents, family friends—ordinary people who lived through extraordinary times.

You'll meet Ratha, my older brother, who wandered from camp to camp as a child, often beaten or starved, who never truly learned how to express love except through protection.

You'll meet Lori, my sister, fierce and defiant, who worked in mobile labor camps and grew up too fast.

You'll hear from my mother, a farm girl in an arranged marriage who lost a daughter and never spoke of it for decades.

You'll learn about my father, whose quiet endurance built a new life for us in Canada, even as he carried unbearable grief.

I am the second youngest in the family. The little brother. The one who, for years, hadn't even known about a sister who had died before I was born. Her name was Po, and she died during the regime—malnourished, like so many children. No one ever spoke of her. Not until I started asking questions. Even then, her memory floated in and out of conversations like a ghost. My siblings remember her vaguely. My father's voice shook when he mentioned her name. My mother could barely bring herself to speak about her at all.

There were no photos. No grave. Just a name, and grief so deep it had been hidden for decades.

That was when I understood the true cost of silence.

For survivors, forgetting is often a survival strategy. You push the past down to move forward. You tell yourself it's over. You pretend, for the sake of your children, that you are whole. But the wounds never fully heal. They simply go unspoken. And the next generation—my generation—grows up feeling something heavy but undefined. We inherit that silence like a family heirloom, passed down in guarded expressions and unfinished stories.

I didn't realize how deep this silence ran until I started these interviews.

I remember speaking with my brother Ratha during our first recorded conversation. He's always been stoic, someone who speaks in short, direct sentences. As kids, we rarely had heart-to-hearts. There was too much distance—emotional, generational, cultural. But when I finally asked him to tell me what he remembers, something cracked open. He spoke of being beaten in front of others. Of stealing rats to roast over open fires. Of crawling back to our parents' camp at night, knowing he might be caught and punished—but unable to stay away from his mother and father.

It was the first time he had said these things out loud. And the first time I truly saw him.

For those of us born during or just after the Khmer Rouge era, we straddle two worlds.

We are Cambodian by blood, but our formative years were shaped elsewhere—in the safe, suburban sprawl of places like Montreal, Windsor, Lowell, or Long Beach. We were taught to be grateful, to work hard, to succeed. But we were also taught not to ask too many questions. Not because our parents didn't love us—but because some truths were too painful to say out loud.

I grew up confused by this.

Why was my father so emotional when we passed by water? Why did my mother get emotional sometimes when she cooked certain dishes? Why were some topics—like our time in the camps, or the journey out—never discussed, even when I asked?

There was no class on how to navigate this dual identity. No school curriculum on Southeast Asian genocide. No children's book on inherited trauma. So we did what children do: we adapted. We became quiet observers. We read between the lines. We listened for what wasn't being said.

And over time, we developed our own version of survival: one that involved code-switching between cultures, decoding silence, and carrying stories we didn't fully understand.

There's a moment in almost every interview I conducted for this book when the person pauses. Their voice breaks. Their eyes drift toward a memory that isn't fully formed but still hurts. That moment is often followed by a deep breath and a quiet "I've never told anyone this before."

That's when I knew I was doing something that mattered.

These weren't just family conversations—they were acts of preservation. And in many cases, of healing. For my siblings, my parents, and others in our community, telling their stories was a way to take back control. To reclaim agency. The Khmer Rouge tried to erase their voices. This book amplifies them.

Some of the stories are hard to read. They should be.

They speak of forced starvation, family separation, abuse, and death.

But they also speak of loyalty, courage, and the will to survive.

What struck me most was the variety of experience. No two journeys were the same. Some were separated from their families and wandered alone. Some found small pockets of kindness in unexpected places. Some lost siblings. Some saw friends killed. Some barely escaped execution themselves. The details are different, but the theme is the same: resilience in the face of unimaginable horror.

Too often, survivors of atrocity are reduced to a single story. We assume there is one narrative: they suffered, they escaped, they rebuilt. But the truth is far messier. Some survivors feel guilt. Others feel anger. Some have forgiven. Some have not. Some want justice. Others want peace and quiet. There is no singular "survivor experience."

This book honors that complexity.

By giving each person a full chapter—in their own words, with their own tone and rhythm—I hope to show the breadth of humanity that existed, and still exists, within our community. These are not cautionary tales or tragedy porn. They are portraits of people who lived through one of the most brutal regimes of the twentieth century and somehow kept going.

And that includes the ones who didn't talk.

Silence, too, is a story.

My sister Vichyini rarely cried. She had learned not to. Crying was dangerous in the camps—seen as weakness. She told me about being exiled to a children's camp for "bad kids," simply for asking for more food. She was twelve. Her story shook me because she carried so much pain with so little fanfare. That, too, was strength.

Or take my father—loquacious, funny, warm. After the war, he went back to school in Canada, riding his bike through the snow to get a drafting diploma so he could provide for us. He started the first Cambodian association in Windsor, helping new arrivals acclimate to their new lives. And yet, in private, he carried the unbearable grief of losing a child. That contradiction—public leadership, private sorrow—is part of his story, too.

There's a Cambodian proverb:

"When the water rises, the fish eat the ants. When the water recedes, the ants eat the fish."

It speaks to power, reversal, and the cyclical nature of fortune and suffering. In Cambodia, power has always shifted, sometimes violently. The Khmer Rouge era was a time when the ants rose—and devoured.

But now the water is receding. And we must decide what to do with what's been uncovered.

When I began this journey, I thought I was documenting the past.

I thought I was assembling a historical record—one that could help fill in the blanks my family had quietly left behind. I thought this would be a work of memory, preservation, perhaps even tribute.

But as I wrote, something deeper happened.

The book stopped being just about history.

It became about healing.

For decades, we had lived beside each other as a family but not always with each other. Our griefs were private, our losses unnamed, our stories held close to the chest like something too fragile to speak aloud. In writing these chapters—listening, asking, witnessing—I finally stepped inside those silences and found my family waiting on the other side.

This was not just an exercise in remembrance.

It was an act of reconnection.

One of the things that struck me most during the interviews was how each of us had lived through completely different versions of the same event.

My father remembers his leadership at the factory, the night fishing, the loss of his daughter, and the constant pressure to protect and provide. My mother remembers the physical pain of childbirth in the jungle, the grief of her baby girl dying in her arms, and the spiritual strength she leaned on to survive. Ratha remembers punishment, hunger, and the burning need to stay close to family even when rules forbade it. Lori remembers movement—always being on the road, always being watched, always aware that even as a child, she had to act like an adult to survive.

And I—well, I remember the quiet.

Not the sound of bombs or shouting. Just the atmosphere. The air in our household. The undercurrent. The mystery.

That was my inheritance: the aftermath.

The ache that never spoke.

Writing this book was not easy. At times, I doubted myself. I worried that I was reopening wounds, that I was taking too much from people already forced to give so much. But every time I considered stopping, someone would say, "This needs to be told." Not for them. For their children. And their children's children.

Because memory fades.

Because documents disappear.

Because entire histories can be erased if we don't write them down.

I was never supposed to write this book.

I wasn't trained to do this kind of work—digging through trauma, documenting memory, carrying the voices of others. My academic and professional life took me into engineering, leadership, operations. Yet somehow, here I am—piecing together a story decades in the making. Not because I had to. Because I couldn't not.

It started as a family project. Something small. A way to preserve stories for my children—so they'd understand where they came from. So they'd know that their grandparents and aunts and uncles were not just survivors, but whole people. Complex. Brave. Broken. Resilient. And through that process, I realized these stories weren't just for my family. They were for anyone who ever asked:

What really happened in Cambodia?

What does survival look like after genocide?

What do we do with the silence we inherit?

One of the most difficult things about writing this book was accepting that truth doesn't always come in full sentences. Sometimes it came in fragments. In contradictions. In long pauses followed by "I don't remember," which I came to understand really meant, "I remember too much."

Trauma doesn't follow a neat timeline. Some of my siblings remembered dates. Others didn't even know how old they were during the war. My parents sometimes contradicted each other. Not out of deceit, but because when you live in survival mode, time warps. Memory dislocates.

So I stopped looking for precision and started listening for truth in the emotion—in the tremor of a voice, the clenched jaw, the way someone hesitated before describing the taste of food they had to steal to stay alive.

That is the truth I've tried to preserve here.

This book is not an encyclopedia. It is not meant to be the definitive historical record of the Khmer Rouge era. Scholars and historians have written volumes, conducted interviews, and archived testimony. But there is something different—something deeply human —about hearing a story from someone who lived it and never intended to become a symbol or statistic.

That's what you'll find in these pages.

You'll see a boy (Ratana) remember the screams from inside a temple used as a prison.

You'll meet a sister (Lori) who became rebellious in Canada, not because she was ungrateful, but because she had learned not to trust authority.

You'll hear from my mother, who could barely speak about her trauma but still smiled when she cooked the dishes that reminded her of home.

Each story is personal. Ground-level. Told in their voices, shaped by their wounds.

If you're looking for heroism, you'll find it—but not always where you expect. Sometimes heroism was in refusing to die. Sometimes it was in protecting a sibling. Sometimes it was in enduring without losing your humanity.

If you're looking for closure, you may not find it here.

But if you're looking for connection—for a window into one of the most devastating chapters of the 20th century, as seen through the eyes of those who survived it—then this book is for you.

The Cambodian genocide is one of the most under-told atrocities of our time.

It often falls in the shadows of better-known genocides—Rwanda, the Holocaust, Bosnia. And yet, it left an entire country gutted. Families erased. Cities emptied. Culture nearly extinguished. The Khmer Rouge didn't just kill people. They tried to erase memory, language, religion, family. They tried to unmake what it meant to be Cambodian.

But they failed.

The fact that I'm here—writing this, in English and in the USA—is proof of that failure. The fact that my siblings raised families, found careers, and still carry our culture is proof. The fact that Cambodian communities exist around the world, rebuilding what was lost, is proof.

We carry scars. But we carry stories too.

And stories are powerful.

They remind us. They ground us. They resist erasure.

This book is a way of saying: We were here. We lived. We remember.

It is for my children, who will never know what it felt like to live under the Khmer Rouge, but who carry that legacy in their blood.

It is for others like me—second-generation survivors—trying to make sense of their identity in the space between past and present. And it is for you, the reader, who has chosen to bear witness.

The chapters ahead will take you into labor camps, rice fields, jungles, refugee camps, and Canadian neighborhoods where survivors tried to start again. Some stories will break your heart. Others will make you pause and breathe deeply. Some are told with warmth, even humor. Others carry anger that still lingers.

None of them are simple.

But if you read them with an open heart—with compassion, patience, and humility—I believe they will stay with you. Long after you've turned the final page.

Because what's beneath the killing fields isn't just blood and sorrow.

It's humanity.

It's memory.

It's a people who refused to be forgotten.

Their stories are not linear. Trauma rarely is. But woven together, they tell a larger truth—not just about what happened in Cambodia, but what happens after. After the war ends. After the world forgets. After the headlines fade.

That's where the real story begins.

When I began this journey, I thought I was documenting the past.

I thought I was assembling a historical record—one that could help fill in the blanks my family had quietly left behind. I thought this would be a work of memory, preservation, perhaps even tribute.

But as I wrote, something deeper happened.

The book stopped being just about history.

It became about healing.

Preface: Navigating the Crossroads of Identity

Mom and younger brother, refugee camp, date 1980

THE EARLIEST MEMORIES I have after arriving in Canada were from my kindergarten days at DeSantis Elementary School in Windsor, Ontario. At the time, my family was living about a block away in a small two-bedroom home. For my five siblings—two older brothers (Ratha and Ratana), one younger brother (Steve), and two older sisters (Lori and Vichinyi)—it must have felt cramped as they had to share a room. But for my younger brother and me, we were fine, as we slept in the comfort of our parents' room. I shared the bed with them, while my brother slept in his crib.

I vividly recall my first day at school, which didn't go well for anyone but me. I was very attached to my family, and when they dropped me off at school, I couldn't stop crying. It must have been painful for the poor teacher, whose name escapes me now. Eventually, they ended up calling one of my family members to take me home—a win for me. I also remember making my first friend, Randy, and the joy of having someone to connect with. Although Randy and I didn't stay friends for long as his family moved after our first year of kindergarten, I can still vividly recall us playing together in the sandpit. It was nice to make a friend, even if it was fleeting. After Randy moved, I can honestly say I didn't have any other close friends until the fourth grade, when my family moved to Lasalle, a small suburb outside of Windsor. There, I met my best and longest friend, Ryan, who remains a close friend to this day.

One memory that stands out from those early years is of the church group that took us in. They weren't our official sponsors, but they became part of our support system, bringing food and clothes, helping my parents, and even watching over my younger brother and me when needed. I remember the day they came to our house and suggested we adopt Canadian names. My brother and I were named after the apostles (even my father changed his name, from Chhan, to John) — a reminder of both their influence and the new life we were stepping into. They felt that we would assimilate better into the school system if we had names our classmates could pronounce. Oddly, only the younger siblings—my younger brother, my younger sister, and I—decided to adopt new names. From then on, I was known as Peter, whereas my given name was Panha (pronounced Pawn-ya). My brother Kosal became Steven, and my sister Sokonni became Lori. I didn't realize it then, but this was the beginning of an identity crisis that would plague much of my life.

Our family moved frequently in those early years. Our second home was larger and hosted even more relatives—cousins and an aunt who were older than me. My younger brother and I remained insepa-rable during this time. I was born in late 1977, and he in early 1980. My next oldest sibling was Lori—ten years my senior. For many years, I didn't understand that gap. It wasn't until my twenties that I learned there was another sister—Poline (we called her 'Po' for short)—who had died during the Khmer Rouge regime. She would have been five years older than me and five years younger than Lori.

As a child, I witnessed signs of that trauma without understanding it. Ratha was reclusive. He mainly stayed in his room, rarely came out, and would have sudden fits of anger. It frightened me and my younger brother. Lori was different—she displayed her emotions more openly. If she was hurt, it often came with tears and an undercurrent of anger or defiance. I didn't have a typical sibling relationship with them, and for years I struggled with that absence, even resented it.

Now, I understand why.

They were still healing. Still surviving.

At school, I felt more Canadian than Cambodian. English became my first language. I was accepted by my peers, and the culture felt familiar. But at home, things were different. My parents and older siblings spoke Cambodian, followed Cambodian customs, and lived with a history I didn't fully understand. I felt like an outsider in both worlds. I didn't speak the language fluently, didn't know the traditions, and sometimes didn't feel like I belonged to either identity.

The turning point came in my late teens, when I began to sense that this internal conflict was more than just teenage confusion. It was shaping who I was and how I moved through the world. I began to seek out the parts of myself I had long ignored—the Cambodian side. It's been a long process, and one that continues to this day.

Writing this book is part of that process. It's a way to reclaim the history I never lived but which shaped me nonetheless. It's helped me reconnect not just with my culture, but with my family. I now talk to Ratha more than I ever have. We message each other often. He's currently battling stage 4 cancer—it's spread to his lungs, throat, and brain. He tells me about his hospital visits, his treatments, the pain. Sometimes he pushes back when we try to comfort him—"Unless you go through this," he says, "it's hard to understand." But I try. I try because I finally see him, not just as my older brother, but as someone who survived unimaginable hardship and carried that silence for decades.

And it's not just Ratha. Through this project, I've begun to hear the voices of all my older siblings—Lori, Ratana, even glimpses of Po, the sister I never met. Each of them holds a piece of our family's truth. Each of them was shaped by war, trauma, displacement, and survival.

But this book isn't only about my family. It's about an entire generation—neighbors, elders, community leaders—who carry untold stories inside them. Stories of survival, loss, courage, and endurance. My hope is to document these stories, so they are not forgotten to history. They deserve to be heard, remembered, and honored.

By listening—truly listening—for the first time, I'm finally seeing my family, my community, and even myself with new clarity.

This book is for them.

And for the younger version of me, who is finally learning what it means to belong.

Chapter 2: The Girl Who Kept Moving

Sister Sokonni (Lori) & Ratha, refugee camp, date 1979-80

GROWING UP, my sister Lori was the one I felt closest to among our older siblings. We were ten years apart, but that still made us the nearest in age. And in those early years—before the war scattered our family—that closeness mattered. She wasn't just a sibling. She was a protector, a playmate, and, in many ways, a caretaker.

We used to walk to school together. I was so little back then, barely able to find my way. But Lori was always there, guiding me, hand in hand. Every day, we'd meet at a family friend's house during our lunch break—this tiny place just half a block from school where we were allowed to eat. In those days, teachers let kids wander off for lunch without much oversight. I still don't know how they trusted us to return, but we always did.

Lori would make me something simple—nothing fancy, just a quick lunch—but because it came from her, it meant everything. She made me feel like I mattered. Like I was safe. I remember one afternoon in particular. She didn't show up on time, and I stood outside the house alone, confused, and panicked, tears welling in my eyes. I don't know if I waited five minutes or fifteen—it felt like forever. When she finally arrived, she saw my face, opened the door, and pulled me inside. No questions. Just comfort. That moment stayed with me. Not just the fear of being alone, but the quiet relief that came with her presence. Even back then, I knew I depended on her more than I understood.

As we got older, I saw Lori change. The fire in her grew stronger—she pushed back more, broke a few rules, carved out space for herself. But that fire never made her scary. It just made her feel more real. She was strong, smart, stubborn—and still an amazing cook. Long before recipe books or YouTube tutorials, she somehow figured out how to make the kind of food my brother and I craved: crispy chicken, stir-fried noodles, pasta. The kinds of meals that made us forget, even for a moment, the heaviness of everything else. She still cooks like that today. I keep telling her she needs to share it with the world.

This is her story. It's not just about survival—it's about strength, resilience, and a kind of love that doesn't always need words. She may have kept moving, but along the way, she carried more than her share —and she always made sure I could keep up.

Before the bombs, before the marching boots, before the silence of emptied cities, she was a little girl named Sokonni.

Lori—her name now—remembers fragments of that early life in Phnom Penh like slivers of sunlight cutting through dust. Not full stories, just moments. She remembers her daily routine: English lessons in the morning, Cambodian school in the afternoon, French in the evenings. Her days were long but structured, cushioned by a life of relative privilege. A chauffeur picked her up each morning with her younger sister, Po, by her side. The English teacher was strict. Some afternoons, they'd come home for lunch and take naps—though Lori hated naps. She could hear children playing outside and wanted nothing more than to join them.

She remembers our mom walking her to Cambodian school. Dinner at home. Then back out again to French school. That school, she says, was big and beautiful, filled with French-speaking children. Her ride home came from a family friend—an older man who would later reappear in a more tragic role. He picked her up on his motorcycle and brought her back safely each night.

Lori thinks she was about seven when it all changed.

April 17, 1975. The day Phnom Penh fell.

The memories of that day are blurred, but the emotions remain sharp. She remembers black-clad Khmer Rouge soldiers flooding the streets outside our home. Curious, she climbed a tree that overhung the brick wall to get a better look. Trucks rolled by filled with young men, some standing on the roofs, waving flags and shouting into megaphones. There was cheering. Clapping. Commotion. Some people actually celebrated, believing the war was finally over.

Then, just as quickly, came the order to leave.

"I didn't grab anything," Lori said. "I just remember people running around, throwing things into cars. We had two cars, but you couldn't even drive—too many people in the way."

So, they walked and when night came, slept along the roadside. Once, they laid down on ground where the earth was still loose, only later realizing it may have been a shallow grave. Every home they passed had been ransacked. It felt like the world had already ended.

They weren't alone. Cousins, uncles, siblings, everyone was leaving—or meeting up along the way. The family became a kind of caravan, moving in waves. At one intersection, they met up with our grandmother, our aunt, and a newlywed uncle. That uncle wanted to head north to find his in-laws, but our grandmother refused to leave her youngest daughter. They split up.

. . .

LORI NEVER SAW THEM AGAIN.

By 1976, Lori was in the camps.

Technically, she was too young. Only eight years old. But the Khmer Rouge had already mastered the art of manipulation. When they came to the family, they didn't demand. They persuaded. They told Lori she was strong, capable of helping rebuild the country. They told our parents it would be a source of pride. That Lori would learn discipline. That she'd be taken care of. They framed it as a contribution to something greater than herself.

To a child raised in a culture of respect and obedience, it sounded like a duty—maybe even an honor.

So she agreed.

But going meant leaving Po behind.

Po, her baby sister, just starting school. Po, who had always followed her like a shadow. Po, whose soft voice would rise with excitement the second Lori came home. One time, Lori arrived on a brief visit and found Po surrounded by other children. They had been teasing her. Po didn't flinch. She stood her ground and pointed proudly toward Lori. "That's my big sister," she said. "She'll protect me."

Lori wanted nothing more than to stay.

But by then, she'd already made the decision. Even now, decades later, Lori carries the weight of that choice. She doesn't say it often, but the guilt lingers. The what-ifs. The what-should-have-beens.

Once you were in the system, leaving wasn't simple. Her return trips home were temporary, like fog on glass—there and gone. She told herself the camp would be a place to grow. That Po would be OK. That this was the right thing.

Those were the lies they'd all been fed.

What awaited her in the camp was not pride. It wasn't purpose. It was indoctrination—swift and systematic.

The first few weeks felt like school in name only. "They tried to teach us that Angkar saved us," Lori recalled. "That our parents were backward. That the old world was corrupt. That if we saw someone stealing or questioning authority, we should report them."

The lessons weren't taught with chalk and books. They were embedded into daily routines, disguised as moral truths. Trust no one but Angkar. Loyalty means obedience. Individual thought is betrayal.

Then, as quickly as it started, the "education" disappeared. Books were replaced with baskets. Lessons gave way to labor.

Digging trenches. Hauling soil. Guarding rice fields from birds. Planting endless rows of rice. Each task was grueling, repetitive, and performed under threat.

"If you didn't finish your row," she said, "you didn't eat. But the older kids moved faster. They'd dump more seedlings into your row as they passed, making it longer. I was always last."

The punishment wasn't just hunger—it was humiliation. There was no mercy for the slow. No understanding for the small. The system didn't care how young you were. It only cared that you produced.

At night, they slept on hard floors, often wet from storms. With only two outfits—one to wear, one to wash—Lori sometimes found her clean set stolen, forcing her to sleep in soaked clothes, teeth chattering, sores forming on her skin.

At one point, she was made to cook for fifty children, alone. She had no training, no tools. She burned the rice. She was scolded. She kept cooking, anyway.

And then there were the moments of terror. One day, screams echoed across the camp: A teacher had killed herself. The children ran to see. Lori followed the sound instinctively, until Ratha—also in the area—intercepted her.

"Don't go," he said. "You don't want to see this."

She turned around. She never saw the body. But she remembers the fear in his voice. The urgency. Even now, she wonders what she was being protected from—and what scars he still carries from what he saw.

Eventually, the indoctrination and labor blurred into one thing: survival.

You moved fast. You obeyed. You didn't ask questions. You didn't speak unless told to. You didn't hope.

And if you did all that, maybe—just maybe—you lived to do it again tomorrow.

One day, Lori was pulled from class to be told Po, her beloved sister, had died. "I cried," she said. "I was so sad. And I felt guilty. I had left her."

There had been no warning. No way to say goodbye. One moment, Po was waiting for her sister to return; the next, she was gone—another child lost to malnutrition and exhaustion. There was no hospital with medicine. No treatment. Just a body growing weaker each day until it couldn't hold on anymore.

Lori walked home for the small funeral.

She remembers washing her sister's body, the skin already cool to the touch. She helped dress her. She carried her coffin. These were the final acts of love she could offer. There were no flowers. No photographs. Just silence and soil.

After the burial, something in her hardened—not into anger, but into quiet resolve. The regime had taken her childhood. It had taken her strength. Now, it had taken her sister.

But it hadn't broken her.

One night, after finally finishing her rice row in the dark while the others were already asleep and full, Lori looked up at the sky. Her body was trembling with exhaustion. The stars blinked back at her through the darkness.

"This can't be it," she whispered. "This can't be my life."

The next morning, she ran. But she didn't run blindly. She knew exactly where to find her family. Our parents had never moved far from their assigned area. People always seemed to know where they were, even under the Khmer Rouge.

But something was missing. And the absence was unbearable.

Po was gone.

The guilt lingered. It always would. She had gone to the camp believing she was doing the right thing—helping her family, helping her country. But in the end, she had left Po behind. And Po had died without her.

"If I had stayed," she wonders even now, "would Po have lived?"

That question lives in the spaces between sentences. In the way she pauses when asked about the past. In the way she carries herself—strong, self-reliant, but never sentimental. That guilt didn't turn her bitter. It turned her inward.

And then, in the middle of all that pain, a new life entered the world.

Me.

Peter.

Her baby brother.

Po died in 1976, and I was born the following year. For Lori, it was as if the family's deepest wound and a fragile new beginning sat side by side. She didn't know how to make space in her heart for both the grief of a sister lost and the arrival of a brother who would never know her — how to reconcile sorrow and renewal in the same breath. "It was strange," she said. "You were so small. And everything was collapsing again. But you were there. Alive. Needing us."

She didn't feel resentment—just confusion. How could a world that took Po give her another sibling in return? How could she protect me when she hadn't been able to protect the sister who had believed in her so completely?

When the Vietnamese invasion began, Lori was with our father. They had left early to find food for the town pig—a mundane task in a crumbling world. But it saved them. As tanks rolled through the countryside and bombs echoed in the distance, they ran home through dust and fire.

Our mother hadn't returned yet. She had gone to work far from the center of town. They waited anxiously, every second dragging like a stone. When she finally appeared—covered in dirt and panic—they barely had time to embrace before realizing someone was still missing.

Me.

The local daycare had already been emptied. Every other child had been picked up hours ago. But when Lori got there, she found me alone. Sitting quietly. Waiting.

She scooped me up and held me close.

"We took you and ran," she said.

Through the streets. Through the confusion. Through a regime on the verge of collapse. My family didn't wait for orders—they gathered what they could and fled. Along the way, a kind woman waved them into a storeroom filled with bags of rice. It was cramped, but safe. For the first time in years, no one was watching them.

Lori looked around at the faces in the room: her parents, her siblings, and now, me.

She had buried one sister. And now she held a brother.

How do you process that as a child?

You don't. Not really.

You carry it.

You survive it.

And maybe, years later, you talk about it.

That night, they slept on the storeroom floor—not in fear of soldiers, but in a silence so new it felt almost frightening. The war wasn't over yet. But something had shifted.

The sounds of marching had stopped.

And in its place, there was the faint, unfamiliar hum of hope.

At last, the family reached a formal refugee camp.

It wasn't home. But it was something.

For the first time in years, the surviving siblings stood in the same place: Ratha, Ratana, Vichyini. Everyone. All still breathing. All still recognizable—barely.

"We were all together again," Lori said.

But it didn't feel the way she imagined.

They were strangers now. Four years of separation, of scattered camps, of lost time—it had built walls between them that even blood couldn't easily knock down. The regime hadn't just scattered their bodies; it had scrambled their memories, dulled their connections, carved up the closeness they might have had.

"I think I saw Ratha twice [while away at the camp]," she said.

"Once when he gave me some rice, and once when he stopped me from seeing the teacher who hanged herself. That was it."

She didn't remember seeing Ratana at all. Or Vichyini. Not even during the escape.

"Even before the war," she added, "we were already in different schools. I remember being with Po. Just Po. We were the closest."

That simple truth cut deep. Po—the sister she had left behind, the one who had believed so fiercely in Lori's ability to protect her—was gone. And now, surrounded by the others, she couldn't feel the connection that Po had always given her without question.

There was no shared mourning. No open grief. Just the quiet reality of survival. No one asked where the missing were. Everyone already knew.

And yet, in the midst of this quiet fracture, something inside Lori began to change.

It wasn't dramatic. It didn't come with a speech or a vow. It began the way most things did in those years: with food.

In the camp, she began helping with meals—not formally, not with fanfare, but out of instinct. Though she had burned the rice when cooking at the camp, she had also learned something. That cooking—even when the food was plain or sparse—was a kind of offering. A form of care.

And now, in a place where families were trying to remember how to be families again, Lori started to reclaim that role—not through words, but through what she made with her hands.

A bowl of rice.

A piece of roasted root.

A gesture of quiet nourishment.

She didn't think of it as maternal. She didn't think of it as symbolic. She just did it. But looking back now, you can see it. The shape of love forming again, not in the absence of pain—but in its shadow.

Especially toward me.

I was still so young. I had no memories of the regime. No images of the camps. But Lori had memories of me—being found alone at the daycare, clinging to our mother, silent in the jungle.

She never said it out loud, but something in her had shifted. She wasn't just my sister. She became something else—something steadier. The one who noticed when I was hungry. The one who knew which foods I liked. The one who, later in Canada, would quietly make me lunch every day while I played, never asking for thanks.

It didn't replace Po. It never could.

But it helped heal something that had been left open.

And it started there in the refugee camp. Where food, once a symbol of scarcity, slowly became a language of care.

CANADA WAS NOTHING LIKE CAMBODIA.

The first time Lori saw snow, it felt magical. Cold on the tongue. Soft underfoot. The quiet blanket of white had a stillness that was completely foreign to her. There were no gunshots. No shouting. No mud. No hunger. The air was clean. The streets didn't smell of sewage. And food—real food—was everywhere.

It wasn't just freedom in theory. It was freedom in every breath. In every bite.

Lori was fourteen when she arrived. Because she didn't speak English, they placed her in a class with students several years younger. But she wasn't embarrassed.

"I was just happy," she said. "Happy to be free. Happy to eat. Happy to have Mom and Dad."

She didn't dwell on what she'd lost—because she didn't know what it meant to have a normal childhood. That concept belonged to other people. Other countries. She had worked in rice fields. Buried her sister. Run through the jungle. Carried toddlers. Survived starvation. Her adolescence had been stripped down to a series of instincts: move, obey, endure.

So when safety finally came, she didn't rebel. She adapted.

Quickly.

She learned English. Made friends. Laughed again. She adjusted to this strange new life not because it was easy, but because she was young enough—and strong enough—to bend.

But there were scars.

She still doesn't like wasting food. She keeps mental inventory of what's in the pantry—just in case. She doesn't ask for help unless it's absolutely necessary. "Even now," she said, "I do things on my own. I don't like relying on people. Because for so long, there was no one to rely on."

Independence isn't a personality trait. It is muscle memory. It was forged in mud and silence and hunger.

In her early adulthood, that independence sometimes looked like rebellion. She stayed out late. Dated. Pushed boundaries. Not out of anger, but out of possibility. Out of the sheer joy of finally choosing something for herself.

"I wasn't breaking rules," she said. "I was catching up."

But even as she pushed forward, the past didn't loosen its grip. Especially when it came to me.

I was the baby during the war. Too young to remember anything. But Lori remembers me. She remembers holding me in the jungle, shielding my thirst with a single drop of water. She remembers sitting beside me on that rock, waiting for the family to find them.

And in Canada, she became my silent guardian by walking me to school and making me lunch.

She may not have said it, but those small acts were her language of love. The same girl who once cooked for fifty starving children in a labor camp, who had cried over burnt rice and stolen clothes, was now making food not just to survive—but to nurture.

To protect.

To care.

I didn't know all of this then. But I felt it. The quiet way she made sure I had enough. The way she looked out for me, even as she carved her own path.

Lori didn't ask for praise. She didn't demand recognition. She just moved. Forward. Always forward. She cooked. She worked. She stood her ground. She did what needed to be done.

Not because she had to.

Because that's who she had become.

She still doesn't chase material things. She appreciates them—but they don't define her. "Food. Shelter. Family. That's what matters," she said. Even now, when she cooks, it's more than a meal. It's a quiet offering to the little girl who once fed children with shaking hands and a growling stomach. It's a way of saying: We made it. We're still here.

She sees this instinct in our mother, too. "Mom still hoards food," she said. "It's instinct. Scarcity does that to you. You save everything. You never throw leftovers away. Because you remember what it's like to have nothing."

She sees it in herself: that fierce independence. That refusal to complain. That deep, unshakable resilience.

And she sees it in Cambodian culture more broadly—the way people guard their resources, protect their families, hold trauma in their bones.

But mostly, she sees it as a gift.

"I think I could survive a lot," Lori said. "I already have."

She doesn't feel broken. Not even haunted. She feels made. Forged. Sharpened. She feels like a tree that kept growing even after the fire passed through.

And when asked what she'd tell future generations—those who've never known war, who may never understand what survival really means—she doesn't hesitate.

"War is terrible for kids," she said. "Nobody really knows what children go through. Nobody sees what stays with you. But if you get through it, you learn what matters. Not things. Not stuff. Food. Shelter. Family."

Then she paused.

"And you learn to move on. Because you have to."

Chapter 3: Ashes in the Rain

My brother Ratha Chhim, date and location unkown

I WOULDN'T SAY I was especially close to my older brother Ratha growing up. He kept to himself, mostly—quiet, private, almost like a shadow drifting in and out of the house. His room was a fortress of silence, the door always closed, the hours inside unknowable. He rarely spoke, never sought out deep conversations, and didn't offer the kind of guidance or attention some older brothers might. And yet, even from a distance, I always sensed he was watching.

There were flashes—rare but unforgettable—when that watchfulness turned into action. He would take me and my younger brother Steve to rent video games, wordlessly pulling out his wallet every time. No complaints. No hesitation. Just action, as though protecting us extended even into the small pleasures of childhood. I never realized until much later that this was his way of showing love—through deeds, not words.

One afternoon, his silence gave way to a different kind of protection. Steve and I were very young, barely in elementary school. We had been tormented by a neighborhood bully, a boy who turned cruelty into performance. He sprayed me with our own garden hose, laughing while I stood there soaked and humiliated. Before I could react, Ratha emerged, swift and unflinching. He grabbed the boy and kicked him so hard he tumbled down the street. That bully never bothered us again.

But what stayed with me more than the kick was what followed. Minutes later, the boy returned with his father, pounding on our door and demanding that Ratha come out and fight. Steve and I dove under the couch, our hearts pounding. My father answered instead, and Ratha stood beside him—calm, steady, unafraid. My father explained, and in a surprising turn, the man eventually backed down, even apologized. It was the first time I understood that Ratha, though distant, was our defender. He bore the quiet weight of protection, even when it went unseen.

Years later, when I finally sat across from him to hear his memories of the Khmer Rouge, I recognized that same protective presence. Only this time, it wasn't about bullies or garden hoses. It was about survival. It was about a boy, barely ten years old, forced to witness humanity's collapse and carry it in silence for decades.

Ratha was the first sibling I interviewed for this book. His voice— raspy and weakened by cancer treatments—trembled at times, but he spoke with a directness that left no room for embellishment. For the first time, he peeled back the mask he had worn his whole life, letting the buried truth escape in fragments.

Before the Khmer Rouge, Ratha's memories are few but warm, like scattered fragments of a childhood that might have been. "We had a chauffeur," he recalled. "We went to school—Cambodian in the morning, French at night. We had everything. We didn't know we were lucky." He remembered holidays by the ocean, the smell of food wafting through the house, and the joy of playing outside in the rain. There were neighbor children too—one boy and one girl who lived across the way. "We used to play together," he said, almost as though reaching for their faces through fog.

He remembered little about extended family, only that Mom's side was poorer and some relatives stayed with us. He was still too young to understand the divisions of class or the weight of history. Childhood was still whole then—until it wasn't.

The end came not with gunfire at the door, but with voices. Trucks rolled through Phnom Penh with loudspeakers strapped to them, Khmer Rouge soldiers shouting that everyone had to leave immediately. "They said it was only for a few days," Ratha told me. "They said they were cleaning the city and we could come back." He paused here and gave a small, bitter laugh—not because it was funny, but because the lie was so obvious in hindsight. "We believed them."

The family obeyed, like everyone else. Neighbors poured into the streets carrying what little they could. Adults whispered to each other, debating where to go. Some suggested heading north, toward where the Khmer Rouge had come from, hoping it might be safer there. But nobody knew. The only certainty was movement—shuffling forward with the masses, trusting that following the crowd was better than standing still.

At first it felt like an exodus without destination, bodies pressed together under the sun, the sound of sandals scuffing pavement the only rhythm. Then the horror revealed itself in scattered flashes along the way—a body lying still by the roadside, a burned-out car smoldering in the distance, the cries of children rising and falling through the crowd. "That's when I knew," Ratha said softly. "We would never see home again."

He was ten years old. A boy suddenly thrust into a world where survival replaced childhood, and ghosts began to follow him.

When Ratha reached the camps, childhood ended. Families were separated with deliberate cruelty. Only the very young—five and under —were allowed to remain with their mothers. At ten or eleven, Ratha was considered old enough to be torn away. He was grouped with other children and placed under the control of a "Bong"—a word that normally meant "older brother" in Khmer but in the camps meant something darker: authority.

"The Bongs had the power," Ratha explained. "Better food, less work, a real bed to sleep on. They gave the orders. If you wanted anything—like permission to go home for a day or two—you needed the Bong to like you." Some children were granted those visits once or twice a year, but only if they kept on the right side of their Bong. For most, it was never allowed.

Discipline was constant and humiliating. When Ratha tried to run away to see our parents, he was caught and turned into an example. "They tied me up and sat me on the ground all night. No food. No sleep. Just tied up until morning. The message was: this is what happens if you run away." He wasn't beaten that time, but the punishment wasn't about pain. It was theater. A warning staged in front of every child to make resistance unthinkable.

Punishments came in many forms—sometimes beatings, sometimes deprivation—but always carried out in front of others. A single child's suffering was a tool to control the group. For Ratha, even one night bound and starving stretched into eternity, humiliation searing deeper than hunger. "They wanted everyone to see," he said. "They wanted everyone to know if you ran away, you were going to pay for it."

Daily life in the camps was built on exhaustion. Children woke before dawn, marched to the rice fields, and worked until dark. Meals were little more than thin soup, often cooked by children too young to know how. "It was just salt and onion leaves, sometimes," Ratha remembered. "No rice. No oil. No meat. Sometimes it made us sick, but you had to eat it anyway."

He paused and added, almost with a grim smile, that when rice was available—even half-cooked rice sprinkled with onion leaves and salt —he preferred it to the watery soup. "At least with rice, you could chew," he said. Quietly, the children would whisper an old saying to each other: the soup they made for us tasted worse than the one for pigs. It was a dark kind of humor, a way to share their misery without being heard.

Hunger reshaped what was possible. During harvest season, when rice fields were nearly ready, children were sent out to catch rats—officially to protect the crop, unofficially to survive. "We had to bring the heads back," Ratha explained, "as proof we caught them." The bodies became food. Roasted over small fires, rats became protein, the charred meat stripped to the bone by starving hands. And it wasn't only rats. "We ate everything," he said. "Scorpions, snakes, crickets, birds. Anything that moved."

Even the Khmer Rouge encouraged vices to control the children. Every month or two, they issued bags of tobacco—not to nourish, but as currency. Too young to understand, the children rolled it into leaves and smoked. "Ninety-five percent of the kids smoked," Ratha admitted. Addiction became just another layer of survival, numbing hunger and masking fear.

Even rest was precarious. Sleeping huts were battlegrounds of territory, each child marking space with what little they had. Without belongings to claim a spot, you risked being pushed out to the margins —half outside, soaked by rain, bitten by mosquitoes. Conflicts broke out constantly, and the Bongs didn't stop them. "They liked to see us fight," Ratha said. "It made us weaker." Survival became not only against the Khmer Rouge, but against hunger, cold, and even other children.

Some nights, Ratha couldn't take it anymore—the hunger, the silence, the separation. He would slip away from the camp and into the jungle, walking for hours until the glow of campfires was far behind him. These escapes weren't rebellions so much as desperate acts of survival, ways to breathe for a moment outside the suffocating order of camp life. "I would go into the jungle. Alone. Hide for a few days," he said. He carried matches, sometimes tobacco, and lived on fish, fire, and whatever he could scavenge.

But the jungle was no sanctuary. It was terror. The trees towered overhead, their thick, hairy trunks looming like guardians of another world. Darkness came quickly, and with it came fear—not just of soldiers or wild animals, but of ghosts. "That's all we heard back then," Ratha explained. "That ghosts lived in those big, scary trees. Even now, I wouldn't dare walk through a jungle like that at night."

He said that as a child, he wasn't afraid of capture or even the wild animals—he didn't know enough to be. What he feared were the spirits people whispered about, the ghosts said to haunt the hairy trees. "Walking in the jungle, all I could think of was ghosts," he told me. "Young or old, everyone talked about them. Some even left offerings— incense, flowers, food—in little boxes at the base of those trees." His voice grew quieter. "I swear, if I had ever seen anything in white clothing move through those trees, I would have passed out or dropped dead on the spot."

That fear was absolute. It clung to him more tightly than hunger, more deeply than exhaustion. To walk alone in the jungle at ten years old was to balance between two terrors: the known cruelty of the camp and the unknown spirits in the dark. And yet, time after time, he chose the jungle.

He described one evening in particular, when he was about ten or eleven. He had run away again, determined to reach our parents before the light vanished. "It was around five o'clock," he remembered. "The sky turning dark, the trees closing in." Every rustle felt like an unseen presence, every shadow another reminder that he was utterly alone.

That was when he saw her.

A Bong—the leader of his children's group—hanging from a tree branch, her body suspended in the fading light. "I only saw her back," he said. "Not her face. Thank God. If I had seen her face, I think I would have lost it completely." Even decades later, telling the story gave him goosebumps. His hair stood on end as though part of him was still trapped in that jungle, walking between life and death.

It wasn't only the sight of death that scarred him, but what it meant.

If even a Bong—someone with perks, better food, lighter work—chose to end her life, what hope was left for the rest? At ten years old, Ratha already understood a cruel truth: sometimes survival meant silence, meant moving forward even when your body screamed to stop.

He whispered prayers into the darkness, calling out to unseen spirits for protection. Each step was a negotiation between the terror of ghosts and the more immediate fear of being caught. "I was so young and so scared–no one was there to help me" he repeated, "but somehow I kept walking."

When he returned to camp, punishment awaited him again. The guards tied him up in front of the others—not beaten this time, but left without food or sleep, sitting bound until morning. The punishment was not the ropes themselves but the humiliation of being displayed as an object lesson. "They wanted everyone to see," he said. "They wanted everyone to know what happens if you try to run away and come back."

That cycle—escape, terror, punishment—became part of his childhood rhythm. The jungle gave him moments of solitude but also its darkest memory. And the camp made sure he never forgot who held power.

Among the many punishments, nights in the jungle, and memories of fear, there was one wound that never healed for Ratha: the death of our younger sister, Po.

"She was the best of us," he told me. It was the first time I had ever heard him speak her name aloud. His voice cracked, and he admitted through tears: "Ah Po was my only best friend I had at that time—and she happened to be our sister. She understood me, never judged me, and loved me, and all of us, unconditionally. Tears just come out every time I talk about her or even hear her name. I guess I will never, ever have closure with that kid."

Po was only three or four when she died—too young to be separated into the camps like the older children. She stayed with Mom and Dad, always close to our mother's side. Ratha remembered her as bright, loyal, and surprisingly strong for her age. "She was smart," he said. "Sweet. She never complained, even when she was clearly starving. She never said, 'I'm hungry.' She just waited for food, trusted it would come."

And she was generous in ways only a child could be. "She would never eat all of her meal," Ratha recalled. "She always saved some in case one of us came home to visit." On one rare occasion when he returned with legitimate permission, Po quietly handed him the food she had set aside, ensuring he had something to eat. She often ate just enough to keep going, leaving the rest for others—Mom, Dad, or a sibling who might appear at the door.

When Ratha snuck home against orders, she was the only one who knew. He couldn't risk being seen—if the guards discovered him there, Mom and Dad would be punished. But Po never betrayed him. Sometimes she covered for him, sometimes she simply watched in silence. On those stolen visits, he might borrow a fishing net from the house, using it to survive a few nights alone in the jungle. Inevitably, Bong would find out and warn their parents: if Ratha didn't return to camp, the whole family would suffer. Mom would beg him to go back, and he always did. Those painful cycles repeated more than once, and Po was the quiet witness each time.

Her own body eventually began to swell—arms, legs, and face—the unmistakable signs of late-stage malnutrition, though no one had words for it then. She grew weaker, her laughter fading. Then came the fever, and the collapse. "She was taken to a hospital," Ratha said. "But it wasn't a real hospital. There was nothing they could do." Within hours, she was gone. Mom stayed by her side until the end, while Dad searched desperately for medicine. Ratha wasn't there—he was in the fields. By the time he returned, Po had already been buried.

The grave was shallow, unmarked, and temporary. Years later, when the family tried to return, the site had vanished. The land had been paved into streets and houses. "We lost her," Ratha said. "And we couldn't even remember where. Like she never existed." That disappearance haunted him even more than her death. It was grief without a place to mourn.

The loss shattered the family. Ratha told me that Dad was never the same afterward. "He still worked, still fished, but something in him broke." Mom, on the other hand, kept going—pregnant with me at the time, still working the fields every day. That relentless labor shielded her from the punishments others faced. The guards saw her effort and spared her from the worst, but the toll on her body and spirit was immense.

And yet, she found ways to protect her children in secret. Dad climbed palm trees to gather sugar fruit, which Mom fermented into wine or cooked down into syrup. She wrapped small bundles of food in cloth, smuggling them to her scattered children under the guise of chores. Sometimes, when she spotted Ratha in the fields, she would call him over as if to give instructions. Instead, she pressed a hidden package into his hands—a few spoonfuls of rice, maybe a bit of sugar. "She saved my life more than once," he said.

The grief of Po's death never left, but no one spoke of it—not for decades. It was too heavy, too cruel, too shameful to have survived when she hadn't. For Ratha, her absence was another silence to carry, locked deep inside alongside all the others.

When the regime finally collapsed in 1979, there was no grand announcement, no banners of liberation. It happened quietly. The guards vanished. Checkpoints dissolved. Whispers moved through the camps: the Khmer Rouge was gone. People didn't wait for confirmation—they simply left.

Ratha did the same. "I didn't pack anything," he told me. "I just started walking." Alone, with nothing but instinct, he set out to find our parents, not knowing if they were alive or where they might be. He eventually found them in an abandoned factory building they had turned into a shelter. He hadn't lived with them for nearly four years, and he wasn't even sure they'd still be there. But they were.

For the first time in years, the family was together again—not for a day or a fleeting visit, but fully, permanently. Ratha never described that moment with flourish. He simply said, "They were there." That understatement carried all the weight in the world.

But reunion didn't mean safety. Cambodia was broken—its fields mined, its cities hollowed, its markets empty. "Dad wanted out," Ratha said. "He knew we couldn't stay. It wasn't safe." Rumors spread about families trying to reach Thailand, where refugee camps offered a fragile promise of survival.

The journey was perilous. Smugglers demanded money, border guards shot at those who tried to cross, and landmines littered the paths. "We saw people die," Ratha remembered. "Whole families just disappeared."

And in the middle of this chaos was me—just a newborn.

Ratha told me a story I had only ever heard in fragments, one that had always sounded almost mythic in its cruelty. "We were walking through the jungle, trying to cross," he said. "You were crying. Mom was holding you. But there were soldiers nearby. Thai border patrol, I think. They didn't want people coming in. They'd shoot if they heard something."

Then came the order: leave the baby.

"They told Mom to throw you away," Ratha said, his voice tightening. At first, I didn't understand. I asked him to repeat it.

"They told her, 'Leave the baby. If you don't, we'll all die.'"

But Mom refused. She wrapped me tighter, held me closer, and kept walking. Ratha walked behind her, heart pounding, waiting for the sound of a gunshot. It never came. "You were lucky," he said. "We were all lucky."

Eventually, they crossed into Thailand and found a refugee camp. Compared to what they had left behind, it was fragile relief: food, rules, shelter, a measure of safety. But it was far from paradise. "There was still disease, still fear, still uncertainty," Ratha explained. "Nobody knew how long we would be there. Some families stayed for years."

For the first time in a long while, survival was no longer about avoiding beatings or hiding food. It was about waiting—waiting for resettlement, waiting for the world to decide whether Cambodia's exiles were worth saving.

At last, Canada offered asylum. The family boarded a plane with nothing but donated luggage, tattered shoes, and a suitcase each. No English. No money. No relatives waiting on the other side. Just the promise of safety.

Ratha still remembers the shock of arrival—the gray skies of

Windsor, Ontario, the biting cold, the first time he saw snow. There were volunteers and caseworkers to meet them, but no real roadmap for how to rebuild. "We were starting from zero," he said.

For Ratha, survival did not end in Canada; it only changed form. He entered high school in the early 1980s, a time when immigration was poorly understood and racism was blunt, unfiltered. "Almost every day I had to defend myself on the way to school," he recalled. It wasn't just one group—it came from all sides, white and Black kids alike. Cambodia meant nothing to his classmates; all they saw was his face, his accent, his difference.

Bruce Lee was a global icon at the time, and because of him, many assumed that all Asians knew martial arts. Some mocked him with shouts and noises, while others tried to provoke fights. At first, Ratha was scared. But survival had been drilled into him since the camps—if you showed fear, you lost. So he adapted. He pretended. He postured like he did know Kung Fu, letting the myth protect him. "I just played along," he admitted. Sometimes it still ended in fights—not usually serious, but enough to prove he could hold his ground. The instincts that had kept him alive in Cambodia carried over into Windsor's streets and schoolyards: stay guarded, strike only when necessary.

At home, the challenges were quieter but no less heavy. The family had to learn how to live from scratch: no English, no savings, no networks to lean on. Jobs were menial, paychecks small. While Dad worked long hours and Mom shouldered endless labor, Ratha carried the silence of his trauma—the images of the jungle, the punishments, the loss of Po. Where other teenagers complained about cafeteria food or homework, Ratha remembered eating rats and snakes to survive.

He finished high school and started working right away—sweeping floors in a factory, then enrolling in civil engineering technology because that was what Dad wanted. "I wasn't good at it," he admitted. "But I didn't want to disappoint him." When I asked what he might have studied if he'd been free to choose, he shrugged. "Maybe music." And as always, he let the silence do the rest.

Life outside school wasn't easier. The family needed every extra dollar, so Ratha joined Mom, Lori, and Vichyini in whatever work they could find. Spring through fall, they went out at night to pick worms, rain or no rain. The wetter the ground, the more worms they collected, the more money they earned. On weekends and holidays, they worked the farms—picking tomatoes and beans, sometimes pulling weeds under the hot sun. Ratana and Dad already had full-time jobs, while Steve and I were too young, so it fell mostly on Ratha and the others to fill the gap. For years, this was their rhythm: school, labor, silence, survival.

That was Ratha. He rarely explained himself fully. Silence had become his first language. Yet in the small things—the way he stayed home, smoked in the garage, lingered in his room—the signs of his past were always there. He flinched when voices rose. He never showed affection easily. Anger was the only emotion close to the surface. And yet, when I pressed him, he told me something I'll never forget: "I wasn't affectionate. Still not. But I protected you guys." That was his version of love—defense, action, never words.

In the later parts of his life, Ratha carried not just memories but sharp, unrelenting questions. One of them came up often when we spoke: *Where was the world when Cambodia was burning?* It was not rhetorical. It was an accusation, one he had carried since the days when he walked roads lined with corpses.

He remembered hearing about organizations like the United Nations, the Red Cross, governments with endless speeches and resources. Yet during the years when his childhood collapsed into hunger, punishment, and silence, he saw none of them. No food drops. No medical tents. No soldiers to protect. Just absence. Just silence. "How come they didn't come to help us?" he asked. "And now, I see them everywhere—rushing into other countries, setting up camps, handing out supplies. Where were they when we needed them?"

That silence became part of his anger, but also part of his identity. While classmates in Canada complained about cafeteria food, he remembered eating rats and snakes to survive. While politicians spoke about *never again*, he thought only of the jungle, of the girl hanging in the twilight, of Po's shallow grave erased by concrete. The imbalance of it all became part of his worldview. He did not trust easily. He did not assume anyone would come to help. "We were on our own," he told me. "And the world looked away."

Even now, weakened by cancer, Ratha's anger hasn't fully disappeared. In a cruel symmetry, his illness circles back to those years in the camps. The very tobacco the Khmer Rouge handed out to children as currency and control became a habit that clung to him for decades, carving its damage into his lungs. He knows it. He admits it. But when he says so, there is no bitterness—only the clarity of someone who has lived long enough to stop lying to himself. The war stole his childhood. Tobacco stole his health. Both were forced into his hands before he was old enough to understand their cost.

What the regime took from him wasn't only years of life—it was his emotional language. Childhood is when most people learn how to love freely, to trust, to speak openly about what they feel. Ratha was denied that. Silence became his shield, his survival strategy. Even decades later, in Canada, surrounded by family and relative safety, that silence remained. He was the older brother who smoked in the garage, who stayed in his room, who appeared in photos unsmiling. Present, but always at a distance.

Cancer, strangely, has softened that distance. The voice once hidden behind silence now rasps through phone calls and late-night messages. He sends photos, articles, fragments of memory. He speaks truths he had buried for decades. The mask has not vanished, but it has cracked enough for glimpses of the boy beneath to emerge. After all these years, he is still learning to find his voice.

When I asked if he had ever healed—from the war, from the jungle, from the loss of Po—he paused a long time before answering. Finally, he said: "I learned to survive. That's enough." No sweeping redemption. No neat conclusion. Just endurance. Just a boy who walked through fire and kept walking.

And that is where the title of this chapter comes into focus. Ashes in the Rain. That is what Ratha carried: the residue of a burned childhood scattered through decades of silence, clinging to him even as life went on. Ashes cannot be rebuilt, and rain cannot wash them clean. But they remain as evidence—of what was lost, of what endures, of what memory refuses to erase.

Ratha's legacy is not triumph but endurance. Not healing, but memory. His life is a testament to what it means to keep living when everything around you insists you should not. His survival allowed me —and all of us who came after—to exist. And as he told me once, in a voice stripped of pretense: "Tell them we were just kids. We didn't choose this. We didn't even understand it. And tell them not to forget."

That is his truth. That is his voice. That is the shadow and strength of my brother, Ratha.

Chapter 4: No One Comes
Back From the North

Sitha Mean, Ratha Chhim, Vichinyi Chhim, Lori Chhim,
Peter Chhim, Ratana Chhim in refugee camp, date
unknown

MY SISTER VICHYINI was just twelve years old when the world came apart. At that age, you're not supposed to carry fear in your bones or loss in your chest. But like so many Cambodian children of the Khmer Rouge era, her childhood was abruptly shattered—ripped from its seams by forces far beyond her control. She doesn't remember what she packed the day they were forced to leave Phnom Penh. Maybe a stuffed animal. Maybe nothing at all. She remembers chaos. Running. Adults yelling. Children crying. She remembers helping our mother and father shove anything of value into a small family car before the roads were blocked and motor travel became impossible.

The family didn't know where to go, only that they had to leave the city. Soldiers with megaphones shouted that everyone had to evacuate immediately. So our parents chose what so many did in those frantic days: They returned to their ancestral village—the only familiar place left.

That decision, my sister now believes, may have doomed them to even harsher treatment. In that rural community, people remembered our father. They knew he had held a respectable job in the city—a supervisor at a factory. He spoke French, wore clean clothes, and had sent his children to school. That alone was enough to make them hated. To be literate, to carry yourself with dignity, to have ever known comfort—these became marks of privilege in a world where survival meant sameness, silence, and submission. Even the children were not spared. Vichyini and my brother Ratana were resented because they could read and write. "They were jealous," she said, "because we knew things. And we didn't know not to tell them we could read."

The Khmer Rouge didn't offer explanations. They offered directives. And soon after arriving in the village, our family was fractured. The regime began to separate people—by age, by gender, by perceived usefulness. Teenagers like Ratana were pulled into work camps for older youth. Adults were dispatched to distant rice fields. And the younger children, like Vichyini, were funneled into children's labor camps with no warning and no ceremony.

Vichyini doesn't remember exactly how it happened. One day, she was with her family. The next, she was gone—loaded onto some kind of cart or ferried away on foot, the memory blurred by trauma. "They had guns, Peter," she told me. "You can't push back when they have guns." She recalls being lined up—assigned like livestock—and waking up in a crowded hut made of bamboo. There were no beds. No shoes. No toothbrushes. Just slats of bamboo to lie on. One set of clothes. One ladle of watery rice porridge, twice a day.

The camp was not a place for children to live. It was a place to break them.

As soon as the sun rose, the work began. Children were roused from sleep, regardless of how much rest they'd had. Some were assigned to nighttime "watch" duties—sitting in shifts, alert for dangers or dissent. Then, at first light, they were marched to the fields. "You work in the rain. You work when you're sick. You only stop when you can't stand up anymore," Vichyini told me. She was sick often. "I think I almost died," she said. "Maybe more than once."

Children coughed themselves awake, scratched mosquito bites until they bled, and walked barefoot through soaked fields. When they came back to camp in wet clothes, there were no changes of clothes waiting. They simply slept in the same damp rags, shivering through the night. Unsurprisingly, many fell ill. There were no doctors. No medicine. No rest. And many died. "Some of the kids didn't even know why they were crying," she said. "They just cried until they couldn't."

Missing even a single meal could be catastrophic. The children were fed on strict schedules, and if you missed your turn—because you were sick, too weak to stand in line, or punished—you went hungry until the following day. That meant going to sleep empty, then waking to another day of hard labor with no nourishment in your body. It left you trembling, dizzy, and more vulnerable to sickness. Some children, desperate and starving, turned to theft. That's how meals disappeared. That's how survival turned into betrayal.

Amid this bleak rhythm, Vichyini was given what seemed like a miracle: permission to visit our parents for one night. These visits happened rarely—maybe once or twice a year—and only under strict conditions. For a child starved of family, they were lifelines.

She remembers setting out after the camp's meager evening meal, the light already fading. She was only twelve. Small. Sick. Homesick. And yet she was determined. The jungle path between her camp and our parents' was long, confusing, and menacing in the dark. She had no candle, no lamp, no one to guide her. Just the press of shadows, the hum of insects, and the pounding of her own fear. Every sound became an omen. Every tree loomed like a figure in the night.

"I got lost a few times," she admitted. "I was terrified. But I kept going." She stumbled over roots, scratched her feet on stones, whispered prayers into the dark. The only thing that pulled her forward was the thought of seeing our mother and father again—of feeling, if only for a few hours, like a daughter instead of a prisoner.

By the time she arrived at our parents' camp, morning had come. Her body ached from exhaustion, but she had made it. Relief carried her the last steps. But when she finally saw our family, her joy collapsed into grief. Po was gone.

She had died the day before in a makeshift hospital, too weak and malnourished for even the most basic treatment to help her. By the time Vichyini arrived, our parents had already brought Po's body back to the camp to prepare her for burial.

"I cried and cried," Vichyini told me. She was allowed to wash Po's body, her small hands tracing the frail outlines of her sister's arms and legs. What stayed with her most wasn't the image of the body, but the feeling: "She was so cold," she whispered. The coldness of death clung to her, etched into her memory forever.

The grief was unbearable. She had spent the entire night walking, holding onto the hope of reunion, only to arrive too late. She wanted to stay, to cling to her mother, to remain with Po until the burial was complete. But the rules of the regime were merciless. She was permitted only that single day. By nightfall, she was ordered back to camp—as though grief itself had an expiration date.

That short return—so longed for, so desperately sought—became not a reunion, but a wound she carried for the rest of her life.

Before she left, our mother, still raw with grief, pressed a cloth bundle into her hands: palm sugar, dried rice, a few precious sweets. It was an act of love disguised as food, a way of telling her, I still see you. I still care if you live. Vichyini clutched it as she walked back into the night, tears blurring her vision.

But even that mercy unraveled. Too weak to guard the bundle, she fell asleep in the hut with it by her side. When she woke, it was gone. She spotted the familiar cloth in another girl's hands and confronted her. "That's mine," she said. "My mom gave me that."

The girl denied it. Hungry and desperate, Vichyini took it back and ate it.

The girl ran to the camp leader. In an instant, the food that symbolized her mother's love became the evidence of her "crime." At twelve years old, she was branded an enemy of the people. The punishment was swift and merciless: exile. She was loaded onto an oxcart and sent away—alone—to a harsher camp for "troubled" children. But she wasn't troubled. She was just hungry. Just grieving. Just twelve.

At the new camp, the rules were harsher. The children were more desperate. Some stole from the kitchens. Others foraged for insects or frogs in secret, only to be beaten when caught. There was no mercy. "They worked us to death," she said. "They starved us slowly." She doesn't remember many names. Time and trauma blur the edges. But she remembers one girl—an older girl, beautiful and kind—who took her under her wing. The girl had connections—someone who liked her, someone who protected her. And in turn, she protected Vichyini.

"She gave me food," my sister said, her voice breaking. "She saved me."

This girl, whose name is now lost to memory, did what the regime would not: She saw Vichyini not as labor, not as a number, but as a child.

For three years, they were in the same camp. Working. Surviving. When the Khmer Rouge began to move sick children farther north, to harsher zones where many never returned, the girl warned her: "If you go up there, you won't come back." But Vichyini could barely walk. She was weak, feverish. She wasn't sure she could keep going. Her strength failed her so often that eventually, she was designated for transfer—to be sent north with the other sick children.

At this point in her story, Vichyini paused. The pain was too raw. Her voice had grown quieter with every memory, each one peeling back layers she had spent decades trying to forget. "I don't like to talk about it," she said softly. "It's too much."

But it is in these quiet truths that history lives—not in textbooks, but in memories barely spoken. My sister's story isn't just one of survival. It's a testament to the hidden strength of children forced to carry the weight of a nation's nightmare. In her silence, in her memories, and in the face of all that tried to erase her—she endured. The regime's logic was brutally efficient: The strong stayed to work; the weak were moved farther away—out of sight, out of mind. No one ever returned from the northern camps.

But the girl—her protector—would not let that happen.

She helped my sister avoid the transport. Somehow, they found a cart, maybe pulled by a cow, maybe pushed by others. Somehow, they bought her time—enough to keep her in the labor camps and not sent to die in the north. Vichyini doesn't remember the specifics. But she remembers what mattered: Someone stood up for her when she couldn't stand up for herself.

"If it wasn't for her," she whispered, "I wouldn't be here."

Even with this help, she still hovered near death many times. Fever. Malnutrition. Constant exposure. She was sick for months—possibly years. "I thought I was dying," she said. "More than once."

And still, the rules didn't bend.

If she could stand, she was made to work. Even in rain, even barefoot, even coughing, even when she could barely hold her own body up. There was no option to rest. "Unless you passed out, they made you get up," she said. "There was no choice."

One time, after days of sickness, she was allowed to stay behind. Not because the guards had compassion, but because she was simply too weak to move. She lay on a mat of bamboo, burning with fever, wrapped in the same wet clothes she'd worn in the fields. Someone— she doesn't remember who—left her alone to recover or die.

Then, something miraculous happened.

Our father showed up.

He had walked the entire day, across fields and villages, with no guarantee that she would be there. He had heard rumors—just whispers —that one of his daughters had been relocated to a distant camp. He pleaded with the local commander to let him visit. He begged for his daughter's life. And somehow, he was granted permission for a single night.

When Vichyini saw him, she cried. It had been years. She had assumed he might be dead. In those days, silence and absence often meant death.

But there he was.

He had brought food. Not much—just what he could carry, what he could trade for, or what little they'd saved. He shared it with her freely. And, just for one night, she felt like a daughter again. Not a prisoner. Not a laborer. Not an accused enemy. Just a child in her father's presence.

"They let me eat," she said, "because Dad was there."

He didn't stay long. He couldn't. Rules were rules, even when they made no sense. The next morning, he had to leave, and Vichyini had to stay. "I cried and cried," she told me. "But he couldn't take me. He just walked away."

She never forgot that walk. Never forgot the image of our father—a man broken by war, but never by love—leaving her behind because the system would not allow mercy.

From that point on, Vichyini said she tried not to feel anything. Emotions made things harder. Missing her parents made the hunger worse. Hoping for kindness made the cruelty sharper. She retreated inward. Survived by following orders. Worked when she was told. Stayed quiet when she was scared.

"I don't think I ever got beaten," she said. "I was too scared. I just did what they said."

Others weren't so lucky. She remembers the sounds of whippings —loud and brutal—and the way children flinched at every crack of a branch or shout of a guard. She remembers the looks on the boys' faces when they were dragged away. She remembers the night screams. The sobbing that never stopped.

When she was finally moved again, she was barely a teenager.

It had been years since she'd seen a real bed. Years since she'd had more than a scoop of thin rice soup. Years since she'd gone a day without feeling like her body might collapse. But she was alive. And that, in the world of the Khmer Rouge, was its own kind of rebellion.

Near the end of the regime's collapse—when Vietnamese forces began pressing inward and the Khmer Rouge started to panic—many camps were relocated again. The sick were pushed out. The older children were trucked to remote areas. No explanations were given. The chaos was mounting. But Vichyini—still sick, still starving—remained in limbo. Not well enough to be useful, not weak enough to be discarded.

She doesn't know how she survived those final months. She doesn't remember the day the war ended. There was no parade. No announcement. Just a fading of the routine. A lightening of the guards' presence. And eventually, word that it was safe to leave.

She had nothing left but her memories.

When the Khmer Rouge regime began to collapse in 1979, it did not feel like liberation. There was no celebratory announcement, no grand exodus from the labor camps. For most Cambodians—especially children like my sister Vichyini—it simply meant the beatings stopped, the guards disappeared, and the silence that had once felt like fear now became a haunting quiet no one could interpret.

The Vietnamese army entered the country, their arrival bringing an end to one horror but ushering in a new kind of uncertainty. The camps began to dissolve, slowly, messily, without guidance or structure. Some of the children were too weak to leave. Others, like Vichyini, simply drifted—wandering in the direction of what they hoped might be family, familiarity, or even safety. After four years of being worked to the bone, starved, sickened, and moved from place to place, she was not the same girl who had once gone to school in a chauffeur-driven car with pressed clothes and English lessons.

She returned to find our family in pieces.

Those of us who had survived had scattered, some in search of food, others in search of each other. For many families, the post-regime period was just as painful as the war itself. People returned home only to find their homes gone. Parents found children they no longer recognized. The trauma didn't end when the regime did—it lingered, embedded in bones, in nerves, in the hollow places behind people's eyes.

In the months that followed, Vichyini began the slow process of coming back to herself—or at least trying to. She was still just a teenager. But she felt ancient. "I didn't know how to talk to people anymore," she once told me. "I didn't know how to be normal. I didn't know how to feel safe."

Food was more plentiful now, but she ate slowly, guardedly. The idea that you could eat without hiding it was foreign to her. For years, food had been a form of power—something you earned, stole, or were punished for possessing. She flinched when spoken to harshly. She didn't like loud noises. Her body was brittle. Her spirit quieter than ever.

Our mother noticed this immediately. She had always been the emotional pulse of our family—gentle, constant, and fierce in her protection. Throughout the regime, she had done what she could. Smuggled food. Searched for us in the fields. Pleaded with village chiefs. But she couldn't protect us from everything. And seeing her daughter come home thinner, more reserved, more fragile than she remembered nearly broke her.

Vichyini remembers those first few nights home vividly. She had been given a mat to sleep on, a pillow she hadn't had in years. And yet she couldn't sleep. Her body had learned to rest in fear, to stay half-awake in case someone came to take her again. She would lie in the dark, listening for the shuffle of guards, the bark of orders, the sounds of other children weeping or vomiting or coughing themselves into silence.

But the house was quiet. And slowly, she realized that no one was coming.

Still, the damage had already been done.

She was no longer a child who dreamed of schoolbooks and clean clothes. She had seen too much. Felt too much. Lost too much.

At some point, she began to speak less.

The war hadn't stolen her voice, but it had taught her to guard it. In the camps, speaking too much—especially about the past—could be fatal. She had learned to edit herself. To keep stories inside. To smile only when others smiled first. And even after the war ended, she carried that conditioning like a second skin.

Even as our new life began to take shape, the past trailed behind us like smoke.

Vichyini enrolled in school again, but she felt out of place. Her classmates didn't understand her silences. Her body had not yet caught up to the idea that she didn't have to brace for violence at any moment. When the bus system went on strike, she walked two hours each way to school. "No one believed me," she said. "But I didn't mind. I had walked farther before." She was used to endurance.

In that way, the war had built something inside her—resilience, discipline, determination—but it came at a steep cost.

She had to learn everything again.

How to speak freely.

How to rest without fear.

How to trust that when someone gave her food, it wouldn't be taken away.

There were years she didn't talk about what happened at all. Not because she had forgotten. But because she hadn't yet found the language—or the safety—to say it out loud.

When I interviewed her for this book, it was the first time she had spoken at length about many of her experiences. She made dinner while we talked, her voice halting. Sometimes she paused to catch her breath. Other times, she fell completely silent. "I don't like this memory," she said. "It's too much." And yet, she kept going.

She told me about the girl who helped her survive.

About the time she was accused of theft and sent away.

About how our mother risked everything just to sneak her a cloth-wrapped bundle of sweets.

About the time our father showed up, out of nowhere, after walking all day just to hold her for one night.

And about how she cried when he left.

"I was surprised he came," she said. "I thought he was gone."

She talked about the children who died. About the girl who hanged herself in the woods. About the beatings she heard but never received. About how fear taught her to obey, but never to feel safe.

And then, finally, she talked about healing.

Not the kind that comes all at once, with a therapist or a ceremony. But the slow kind. The kind that happens over decades. In the quiet routines of work. In the laughter of her own children. In the moments when she allows herself to sleep deeply. In the strength of knowing what she lived through and how far she's come.

Even now, when she talks about Cambodia, her tone changes. She is proud of our family. But she does not romanticize the past. "I don't want to go back," she told me once. "It's too hard to see the poverty. Too hard to see what the country could have been."

And she has every right to feel that way.

She survived something most people can't even comprehend. And she did it without complaint. Without spectacle. Without ever once crying out loud.

That's who she is.

My sister Vichyini—who once worked in the rain with no shoes, who once shared her only bowl of rice, who once stared death in the face and survived it—not because she wanted to be a hero, but because she simply had no choice.

She didn't ask for this story.

But it's hers.

And now, finally, she's ready to let it be told.

I didn't fully understand how much Vichyini had endured until I heard her try to speak about it. Even now, decades later, the pain still grips her voice. She was a sick, isolated child in one of the harshest camps the regime had, far from family and barely clinging to life. Her memories aren't dramatic—they're quiet, almost subdued—but that's what makes them so haunting. She doesn't talk about being strong. She just was.

But there's one memory that brings emotion rushing to the surface every time—our mother. In the midst of that isolation, it was the thought of Mom that kept her going. She still remembers the day when Mom crossed a lake—risking everything—carrying food wrapped in cloth, not even knowing for sure if Vichyini would be at the other side. That simple act—a mother's blind hope, her desperate love—became a turning point. It wasn't just the food that nourished her. It was the proof that someone still saw her, still cared if she lived.

That moment etched itself so deeply into her soul that she's never let it go. To this day, she lives with a quiet sense of devotion. She shops for Mom's groceries, supports her financially, and once even tried to buy her a home—just to show her gratitude in the only way she can. For Vichyini, surviving wasn't just about enduring. It was about holding onto love. And it was that love—especially the love of our mother—that saved her.

Chapter 5: The Boy Who Would Not Break

From left: Ratha, Ratana, Chhan/John, Peter, Sitha,
Vichinyi, Lori, refugee camp, 1979-1980

GROWING UP, I wasn't especially close to Ratana. He was the eldest sibling, and I was near the youngest—nearly two decades apart. We weren't emotionally distant, just living in different phases of life. By the time I was in elementary school, still figuring out lunch breaks and playgrounds, Ratana was already deep in the adult world—working, married, raising a daughter.

But I always watched him. Even as a kid, I could feel the quiet intensity with which he moved through life. He was the first of us to marry, the first to buy a home, the first to start a family. And when that life unraveled—when his first marriage ended and he lost the house—he didn't break. He returned to our parents' home with his daughter and started over. I was there. I saw the exhaustion on his face, the weight he carried, and the quiet resolve that kept him moving.

He went to work. He went to school. He raised his daughter with every ounce of strength he had. He never asked for sympathy. He never made excuses. He just did what needed to be done—for his daughter, for himself, for the future. Watching that kind of devotion left a permanent mark on me. It showed me what responsibility looked like—not in words, but in action.

Later, Ratana remarried and built a new chapter of his life with grace and purpose. He and his wife from Cambodia had two more children—a son and a daughter—and I've seen the same unwavering love in the way he's raised them. He built a family twice over, carrying the lessons and love forward with quiet consistency.

These days, I hold more degrees than I ever imagined—an MBA, a PhD, and more. On paper, it might look like I've surpassed him. He's even said so, casually, as if I'd gone further than he ever could. But what he doesn't realize is that his story is stitched into every page of mine. I watched him hold his family together through heartbreak. I watched him rebuild, without complaint. That gave me strength. It gave me direction.

This may be the first time he's hearing it, but Ratana was one of the biggest reasons I kept going—through school, through setbacks, through every moment I wanted to give up. His strength taught me what was possible. His love for his children showed me what mattered most.

So, Ratana, if you're reading this, know that I've always looked up to you. Not just for surviving the war, but for everything that came after. You didn't just endure—you built. And in doing so, you left all of us a quiet, powerful legacy.

Before the world fell apart, Ratana lived a life of privilege and warmth. He was born in May 1961, the eldest of us all, and in those early years, he was the golden child—not just to our parents, but to anyone who knew him. His was a charmed childhood, filled with doting grandparents, swimming outings, colorful markets, and the hum of a family still intact.

He spent much of his early life living away from home, embraced by extended relatives who adored him. For two years, he lived with our grandparents. He was with our grandfather when he died in 1972— Ratana was only 10. That loss, the first major fracture in his young life, came just before the greater collapse that would follow. After returning home briefly, he was sent to live with our uncle, who would later move to Paris. But no matter where he was, Ratana was never short on affection. Each home offered care, laughter, and new worlds to explore.

"I had a good life, you know? Before everything changed. People loved me. I was the first-born—so everyone wanted a piece of me."

He returned to our immediate family just before Khmer New Year —an act of fate, in hindsight. The Khmer Rouge came to power soon after, and had he not made it home in time, there's no telling if we ever would have seen him again.

That flight back, riding a commercial transport plane packed with rice and cargo instead of passengers, was a prelude to the chaos ahead.

"It was a strange flight. I was twelve, sitting on bags of rice and boxes. Like the world was already starting to feel unstable, even before the soldiers came."

In those final months before the collapse, Ratana lived with joy and mischief. He had access to things most Cambodian children didn't— rides from chauffeurs, outings with our father's boss to go swimming or fishing, even rides on a Ski-Doo. He was especially close with a cousin who doubled as his best friend. Our house was crowded, and he loved it. More people meant more stories, more jokes, more warmth.

He snuck off to arcades after school, had money to spend, and thought himself untouchable. He was clever, rebellious, and a bit of a charmer. Dad spanked him often, but it rarely stuck, because Ratana believed he could talk his way out of anything. And more often than not, he could.

"I wasn't afraid of getting in trouble. I figured I'd always find a way to talk my way out."

At thirteen, just shy of fourteen, he stood on the cusp of another life milestone: an arranged marriage. The girl was a schoolmate. Their families were close. It was a traditional match, decided by adults, with the kind of formality common in Cambodian households at the time.

"We were supposed to be married. Her family liked ours. We were kids, but that's how things were done. Then—boom—Khmer Rouge came, and that was the end of that."

Everything fell apart.

The regime came swiftly. His fiancée's family scattered like dust. Years later, long after the war ended, she returned and tried to find him. But too much time had passed. They had become strangers.

During the occupation, Ratana was assigned to a youth labor camp. His rebellious spirit didn't vanish—it sharpened. He saw the cruelty of the Khmer Rouge for what it was: senseless, violent, degrading. And while many tried to survive by becoming invisible, Ratana had never known how to shrink. He refused to submit quietly.

"I hated the unfairness. They punished you for being human."

One night, they came for him.

"They woke me up and said, 'Let's go for a walk.' That's what they said before they killed people. But these guards—they were just kids. Little kids. Could barely hold their rifles. When we got to the edge of the woods, we jumped them. Beat them. Ran back."

And Ratana returned to the camp—alive.

The next morning, the camp supervisor was stunned to see him standing there. They couldn't kill him openly now, not after that spectacle. So they resorted to something more insidious: starvation.

"They were shocked we came back. But after that, they tried to starve me instead."

They reduced his rations. Gave him the worst tasks. Isolated him. Tried to make his survival a burden. But Ratana, ever resourceful, found ways to stay alive. He snuck into nearby fields and stole pumpkins under cover of night, cooking them in secret to stave off hunger.

Eventually, he was caught.

"I wasn't trying to rebel. I was trying to eat. But they caught me, and this time, they really tried to humiliate me."

They shaved his head and tied him to a post in the blazing sun. Every person in the camp was forced to walk by and look at him. The guards pointed: "This is what happens when you rebel." "This is the bad child." It was psychological warfare disguised as discipline.

And then, something even worse happened.

"They called me the bad kid. Made me an example. Even Vichyini saw me. She walked by crying. I couldn't even lift my head to look at her."

She had been transferred to a neighboring camp and happened to pass through that day. She saw her brother—her protector—tied up, sunburned, and broken. And Ratana, too weak from hunger and heat, couldn't even look her in the eyes. That image stayed with them both.

After that, he was more alone than ever. Marked. Avoided. People didn't want to associate with someone labeled an enemy. He was assigned another hopeless job: tending to a frail, nearly useless water buffalo.

But Ratana turned punishment into opportunity.

They sent him to work the shallow waterways with the buffalo, assuming the labor would break him.

"They thought they were punishing me. But I turned that into something. I used the buffalo near the shallow water to trap fish, turtles, even snakes. I ate good. And I shared it."

Word spread. Slowly, friendships returned. "You feed someone when they're starving, they remember." And in a world of starvation, food was a powerful currency.

The supervisor noticed this popularity—and didn't like it.

Ratana was transferred again, this time to a camp known for breaking troublemakers. A place where "bad kids" went to be reformed through brutal labor and fear.

But Ratana didn't break there, either.

Instead, he adapted. He started talking. Telling stories. Not lies— memories. Descriptions of life before the war. Of homes with running water. Markets with sugar and mangos. Games played in the shade. His voice became a portal to a world most of the kids barely remembered or had never known at all.

"They'd never heard someone describe life before the war. They ate it up. I gave them hope."

The camp leaders noticed. His charisma was dangerous—but also useful. When he was summoned back, Ratana expected another punishment. Maybe worse.

But instead, the supervisor offered him a new role. "You know how to talk to people," they told him.

"That's how I survived," Ratana said. "Not with fists—with my mouth."

He became a kind of messenger. A liaison. He didn't carry a weapon. He didn't beat anyone. He connected people. He translated. And when he could, he helped. Quietly. Cleverly.

"People respected me because I never acted like I was better than them. I just helped."

Ratana had outlived execution attempts, public shaming, starvation, and exile. But his greatest test was still ahead.

One day, while carrying harvested rice to the top of a makeshift platform—the "skylight," they called it—the wooden beams beneath him collapsed. He fell twenty feet, landing hard. His legs, his ribs, his back—everything shattered. He couldn't move. Couldn't speak. The workers assumed he was dead.

There was no stretcher. No help. They dragged his limp body to a tent reserved for the dying. In the Khmer Rouge system, if you couldn't work, you didn't matter. His body was tossed among the old and sick, left to rot quietly.

But the old people saved him.

They gave him what little they had. Shielded him from rain when the tent flooded. Kept him warm. Whispered stories to him like lullabies meant to hold back death. One elder, a man versed in traditional remedies, concocted a strange but potent treatment: boiling water, seven black pepper seeds, and Ratana's own urine.

"I drank it every day for three months. Disgusting. But I didn't care. I just wanted to live."

And it worked.

The swelling eased. His bones began to heal. He sat up. Then stood. Then walked. When he returned to the main camp, people stared.

"They looked at me like I came back from the dead."

Ratana's resilience only grew stronger. He stole food again—this time rice—and was punished once more, publicly shamed and tied. But still, people listened to him. Even the "bad kids" assigned to break others began to follow his lead. When he was transferred again, this time to the harshest youth labor camp, something shifted.

He became their voice.

"Even the kids who used to beat others... they started listening. They saw I wasn't scared of the guards."

He didn't resist with violence. He infiltrated the system with wit, memory, and quiet authority. He told stories of life before the war—of warm kitchens, of music, of games—and gave the children something the regime couldn't take: imagination. They clung to his words like oxygen.

Eventually, his influence couldn't be ignored. He was promoted again, not out of mercy but calculation. The regime recognized his ability to lead, to maintain order, to keep morale from collapsing. He became a courier. A negotiator. He manipulated food tallies to divert rations to the starving. At one stop, he dropped off extra rice with a family friend who cooked for him in return—a small, private rebellion wrapped in kindness.

"They couldn't count, but I could. That saved lives."

Still, he never lost sight of the risks. His popularity made him a threat. But before the Khmer Rouge could crush him for good, the war began to turn.

The Vietnamese invaded. The regime collapsed. Many people fled. But Ratana stayed with friends. Not because he wasn't eager to reunite, but because home no longer felt like something he recognized.

"I didn't know what home meant anymore. My life was built around surviving. Going back felt more dangerous than staying."

Meanwhile, back in our village, nearly everyone had fled—except our mother. She stayed. She didn't know if Ratana was alive, but she refused to leave without him.

"She didn't give up on me. Everyone else left—but not her. That's Mom."

Eventually, Ratana returned.

But peace was short-lived. The Vietnamese began recruiting young men, including Ratana. He was only seventeen when they sent him to a military training camp. He endured drills, gun training, and harsh conditions. But he had no intention of staying.

"They trained us hard—guns, drills, no food. I wasn't about to die in their army after everything I'd already survived."

He escaped. Disappeared into the forests behind our village, armed and ready. He and his friends knew the terrain too well for the Vietnamese to catch them. They hid. Moved. Waited. Survived.

Then came the final chapter of his Cambodian story: the boat.

Our father had secured a medical transport boat. Ratana worked on it, ferrying people, earning money. The boat was spiritual, he believed. When he misbehaved—brought girls on board or acted disrespectfully—it would stall in the water, refusing to move.

"That boat was cursed—or maybe it just had a conscience."

Eventually, they planned to sell the boat in Vietnam, but sensed a trap. They escaped before the deal turned violent. That boat—spiritual or not—became their salvation. It bought them time. It bought them freedom.

Ratana, Vichyini, and Ratha set out together again. They tried to flee through Vietnam, but the ocean route failed. So they returned and took a land route through pirate-infested forests to the Thai border.

The crossing was dangerous. Armed men stalked the woods. Refugees were robbed, killed. And I—the youngest brother—was just a baby. I cried constantly, making the group a target.

"No one else would touch you—you were crying too much. But Mom? She never let go."

With a crying infant in her arms, she walked step by step through the jungle. No fear. No complaint. Just love.

They made it to Thailand. To the refugee camp. At last, safety.

But safety wasn't easy. The camps were crowded, disease-ridden, and rough. Still, for Ratana, it was the first time in years he didn't sleep in fear. No guards. No whippings. No threats.

He could finally breathe.

He didn't talk much about the refugee camp. He was already looking ahead. When the sponsorship came through, they boarded a plane to Canada—and left behind the world of starvation and trauma.

But trauma travels.

In Canada, Ratana began a new life. He worked. He married. He raised his family. But some wounds remained invisible. He smoked his first cigarette in 1977—not for pleasure, but because the Khmer Rouge gave him tobacco instead of food. He used it to trade for scraps of rice. He quit in 1987, a decade later—but the war stayed in his lungs.

"Even when I was safe, I didn't feel safe. That part of me stayed broken."

He rarely spoke about those years. Not at work. Not even to family. Until now.

When I interviewed him for this book, something shifted. He opened up. He laughed about the haunted boat. He smiled recalling the food traps and friendships. He grew quiet when remembering Vichyini crying as she saw him tied to the post.

And he almost cried when he talked about Mom. About how she waited when everyone else left.

Even now, Ratana carries those years with a kind of quiet pride. Not because of what he suffered, but because of what he refused to become. He never turned cruel. Never stopped helping others. He stayed kind in a world built on brutality.

"I wasn't a hero. I just couldn't stand watching people suffer. If I could help, I helped."

He wasn't perfect. He was defiant, stubborn, a bit reckless. But when the world fell apart, he stood tall.

He never broke.

"I think I survived because I never gave up on people. Even when they gave up on me."

And somehow, in the darkest corners of history, he helped others find their light.

Looking back now, I realize Ratana has always been a steady presence, even if he never asked for recognition. He didn't need to be loud to make a difference. He led by example—responsible, loyal, quietly loving. He gave of himself not just to his children, but to all of us. And I know I'm not the only one who learned from him.

He taught me—without ever saying it—what it means to endure with dignity. What it means to protect others, even when you're hurting. What it means to rebuild, again and again.

That kind of strength doesn't fade.

It stays with you.

Chapter 6: The Village Girl Who Carried the World

Sorth Chhim, date unknown

BEFORE THE WAR, before the forced marches, before the unbearable choices, my mother was just a village girl. A girl with soft features, dark eyes, and a laugh that came easily—at least that's how others remembered her. She didn't read or write, didn't carry certificates or diplomas, but she knew how to survive, how to tend a home, and how to love without condition. That was her education, her inheritance.

"I don't know book," she once told me, pressing her hand gently to her chest. "But I know my heart."

Born into a rural farming community, she grew up with siblings and cousins, running barefoot between the trees and fields. The days were long and hot, filled with chores, but also joy—the smell of boiling herbs, the chatter of women weaving palm fronds, the laughter of children playing near the water's edge. My mother's world was simple but intact. She was the kind of beautiful that turned heads in the village—demure, delicate, with a spark in her expression that made her seem older than her years.

She was still a teenager when she was introduced to my father. Their match was arranged, as most were, but by all accounts, she didn't resist it. He was older, educated, a man with poise and vision. My mother, by contrast, had never set foot in a classroom.

"I don't talk much," she said about herself. "But I listen good. I am a good wife."

They married not long after. She devoted herself fully to her role as wife and, soon, mother. In the years before the war, their life was blessed. My father's education in Paris opened doors few Cambodians could even approach. He was multilingual, refined, a rising star in the capital's manufacturing scene. His success afforded them a large home in Phnom Penh. It wasn't uncommon in Cambodia for extended families to live together, and because my father had the means, he brought many in—siblings, cousins, even old neighbors who needed work.

My mother oversaw the home. Her cousin became the family driver. Other relatives helped clean and cook. She was proud of the household she kept, and of the seven children she bore—each one loved deeply, each one a blessing.

"Seven baby I have. All different. But I love all same," she once told me.

Then, in April 1975, everything broke.

The Khmer Rouge swept into Phnom Penh, declaring Year Zero. Cities were emptied. Money was abolished. Families were told they had to leave temporarily—for "re-education," for safety. But no one returned. My parents were among the hundreds of thousands evacuated on foot, in heat and silence, to a future no one could predict and a past no one could bring with them.

Her voice, which trembles at happy memories, begins to shake when she talks about what followed. "I see many people die," she whispered. "Too much crying. Too much hungry."

Her cousin—the driver—left in the chaos to go park the car and never came back. My mother never saw him again. That small loss was the first of many. Her large, bustling household was scattered into the wind.

In those early weeks, she worried constantly—not for herself, but for her children. "What we eat? How we survive?" she would repeat. The march was endless. She carried the youngest, while trying to coax the older children forward. She bartered and begged for food. She scavenged. She cried privately so the children wouldn't see.

They eventually reached a relative's village, hoping it would be safer, more familiar. But safety was an illusion. Soldiers arrived not long after, shouting slogans and demands. Her heart broke the day the soldiers came for her children.

"They say children help the country," she said. "They say it better. But I feel in my heart—no. No good."

All of the children were taken from her, except Po, the youngest— just a toddler at the time. My mother was sent to a nearby women's camp, where she worked ten days at a time before being allowed to return and see Po for one precious day.

This is how they kept the family alive—barely. My mother working without pause, returning to tend to a daughter whose health was failing; my father scraping by in another camp, doing the same. It was survival by patchwork.

"Po... she so small," she recalled, her voice cracking. "But smart. She say, 'Mom, I not hungry.' Then she hide food for me and Dad."

Po's little body began to swell. There wasn't enough food, and she had been eating leaves, tree bark, whatever she could find. The family watched her stomach stretch unnaturally. She grew quieter. Her spirit, still luminous, began to dim.

"I try take her to hospital," my mother said. "But hospital no medicine. No doctor. Just empty room."

The pain of losing a child is not linear. It doesn't end. My mother doesn't like to talk about it, and when she does, it's only in fragments. Her hand moves to her chest. Her eyes go distant. The wound is still there, beneath the surface.

After Po's death, something in my mother shifted. The world had already fallen apart—her children had been taken, her home was gone, and her body pushed to the brink each day under the Khmer Rouge— but now the light inside her dimmed, too. Grief became part of her breath, a second heartbeat.

The regime separated my parents further, perhaps hoping time and distance would numb the grief. It didn't. But they endured.

One of the stories my mother still recounts with clarity is the day she heard rumors that a children's camp had been established nearby. With no proof, no certainty that her children were there, she made a decision. She took the small bundle of rice she'd been given for lunch, tied it in cloth, and set off—toward a swampy lake that stood between her and the camp.

There was no bridge. And she couldn't swim.

"I don't care," she said. "I say, if I die, I die. I want to see my baby."

She walked into the water. The mud sucked at her legs. The water rose to her chest. At one point, she could no longer feel the ground. She panicked, but kept moving, feeling with her toes, praying, sobbing, whispering the names of her children.

She made it across. Exhausted, soaked, shaking—but alive.

She asked around quietly, careful not to draw attention. Then she heard a name: Vichyini.

"She cry when she see me," my mother smiled. "She say, 'Mom!' And I say, 'Shhh, shhh.'"

She gave her daughter the tiny bundle of rice. She hugged her. Then she turned back, retracing her steps across the water, risking everything—including her life—just for a few minutes of love.

This is who my mother was: the woman who couldn't read a map, but found her way through swamps and suffering. The woman who feared drowning, but waded through deep water for the chance to feed her child. The woman who buried a daughter and still had the strength to mother two more.

"She so brave," my aunt once told me. "But she don't know it. She think only of her kids."

They moved my mother again. She was sent to a new women's camp, distant from my father, deeper in the jungle. She didn't resist. There was no use resisting anything by then. The Khmer Rouge didn't operate on reason or mercy. They moved people like chess pieces across a board soaked in fear.

Each day, she rose before the sun. She worked from dawn until dusk—planting rice, hauling water, gathering firewood. The labor was backbreaking. There were no rest days. No breaks. No nourishment. Only whispered prayers and fleeting dreams.

"I cry, but quiet," she said. "If too loud, they punish."

Every ten days or so, she was permitted to return to the makeshift hut she shared with my father—if it could even be called a hut. It was little more than a raised platform with some wooden planks and palm thatch. But it was shelter. It was love. It was all they had.

That's where she got pregnant again.

At first, she was hesitant to believe it. Her body had been starved, her cycle irregular, and the environment around her was hostile to life of any kind. But then the signs came—the nausea, the tightening in her belly, the flutter of something growing inside her. She was terrified, but also... hopeful.

"I think maybe Po come back," she told me once, tears catching at the corners of her eyes. "I dream... she come to me and say, 'Mom, I miss you. I come back.'"

It was the only comfort she had—the belief that her daughter might return, even if in a different form. It gave her strength. A reason to survive.

But the Khmer Rouge didn't care if you were pregnant. There was no leniency, no exemption. She worked every day of her pregnancy, carrying loads, squatting in rice paddies, cooking over open fires. As her belly grew, so did the danger.

By her eighth month, she began to feel the pressure—literal and figurative. The baby was coming soon, and she knew there would be no help. She had no midwife, no medicine, no clean water, no tools. Just her fear. And her determination.

One day, the pain became too strong to ignore. She could feel the labor starting. Her back ached. Her breathing grew shallow. She approached her camp supervisor and pleaded for help.

"I think I have baby now," she said.

The woman looked her over coldly. "If you lie," she warned, "we kill you. We kill baby. We kill your husband."

That was the level of terror they lived under. There was no compassion—only suspicion and punishment.

But my mother wasn't lying. She begged God to protect her and asked the woman for mercy. She was granted one small accommodation: She could work in the cooking station that day—closer to the hut she shared with my father. That way, if the baby came, she wouldn't be far.

The cooking station was brutal. The fire pits belched smoke. The heat was unbearable. The smells made her sick. But she endured.

That night, as dusk fell, the contractions grew sharper. She stumbled back to the hut, where another woman—slightly older, more experienced—helped her lie down. There were no gloves. No antiseptic. Just dirty cloth, calloused hands, and whispered instructions.

"Push," the woman said. "No scream."

And so, in the middle of the jungle, under a thatched roof, with the world still spinning in violence and oppression, my mother gave birth.

"It not Po," she said softly. "It's a boy."

She was surprised. Maybe a little disappointed. But not for long. When they saw that I was healthy—crying, moving, alive—they gave me a name that reflected the hope I carried:

Panha (pawn-ya).

"Smart." "Wise."

In that moment, I became more than a newborn—I became a

symbol. Of continuity. Of resistance. Of life winning, just barely, against death.

But my birth didn't change the rules of survival. Once she was back on her feet, she returned to work. Her body still sore, her muscles still torn. There was no recovery period. Just more labor.

At one point, the family was ordered to relocate again. The war was entering its final phases, but no one knew that yet. As the Khmer Rouge began to fracture internally, conditions in the camps grew worse —more arbitrary, more violent. People were disappearing. Executions increased. Hope was dangerous.

She was still carrying me as they moved through the jungle toward what they hoped would be safety. The trip was long. The terrain was cruel. The nights were colder now.

I didn't make it easy. I wouldn't let anyone else carry me. I cried when separated from her. I wailed if anyone tried to feed me but her. And sound could be fatal.

Some urged her to leave me behind.

"She not strong enough for both," someone said.

"She carry too much. Baby cry too much."

But my mother wouldn't hear it.

"No! Never!" she snapped. "I die first. You don't touch my son."

She risked all of their lives, in some people's eyes. But she didn't see it that way. I was her son. I was her second chance. And no child of hers would be abandoned.

"People think I weak," she told me once. "But I strong when I need."

Even when they finally found shelter at my father's village (where they were initially separated), she thought constantly of the child she'd lost and the ones she still had. Lori. Ratha. Vichyini. Ratana—who was missing.

She barely saw Ratana during the years of occupation. She didn't know if he was alive. But after the Vietnamese liberation and the fall of the Khmer Rouge, the family began to reassemble—fragmented, limping, but intact.

One by one, they returned to my father's village. But not Ratana.

Days passed. Then weeks. My father was ready to leave. But my mother refused.

"No. I wait for my son," she said.

Others had already moved on. But she remained. She told my father they weren't going anywhere until Ratana came back. And eventually, he did.

"He come running," she remembered. "Skinny, dirty, but alive. I hug him, don't let go."

The family, against all odds, was whole again—at least physically. But mentally, emotionally, the scars would remain.

And for my mother, the journey wasn't over. Not even close.

Canada was supposed to be the Promised Land. A place without war. A place where people didn't vanish in the night, where mothers didn't hand over their children at gunpoint, where babies weren't born in shacks to the sound of marching boots. It was supposed to be a second chance—or at least, the start of one.

But second chances don't come easy when you arrive with no money, no education, no English, and seven children in tow.

My mother landed with her family, body worn thin from years of labor, her heart scarred by grief, her spirit still cracked from the war. And yet she kept moving. That's what she did. That's what she always did.

SHE HAD SURVIVED GENOCIDE. Surely she could survive poverty.

In Cambodia, she had been part of a respected household—married to a man who had studied in Paris, had lived in a beautiful home, and was once a general manager in a factory that supported multiple relatives. But in Canada, all of that vanished. No one cared about what you were before. Here, your accent defined you. Your broken grammar defined you. Your calloused hands and hunched back became your résumé.

She didn't speak the language, but she understood what needed to be done. They needed money. The kids needed food, clothes, shelter. So she went to work.

Factory jobs. Farm jobs. Night shifts. Cleaning jobs. The worm farm.

She worked anywhere that would take her.

"I no care if people laugh at me," she once said. "I clean toilet, I cut worm, I cut garlic. I do anything. My kids have food."

She didn't complain. Not to us. She cried sometimes, quietly, while boiling rice or folding laundry. But she never asked for sympathy. Only strength.

We hardly saw her when we were little. My younger brother and I were often alone at home, with occasional visits from relatives who would check in on us between their own shifts. We didn't fully understand it then, but her absence wasn't neglect—it was sacrifice. She traded time for our future.

And that sacrifice took its toll.

Her hands, once delicate, became swollen and stiff. Her knees began to ache. She worked herself into the ground, until her body finally pushed back. Arthritis came like a thief, stealing her ability to stand for long hours or grip things tightly.

By the time I was in middle school, her pain was constant.

But she didn't regret it.

She had raised a family in the middle of a war, carried children through jungles while pregnant, risked her life to sneak across lakes just to catch a glimpse of her daughters. Working sixteen-hour days in a cold country was just the next chapter of endurance.

"I not smart like your dad," she told me. "But I strong. I live for you."

That strength shaped everything I knew about motherhood. She wasn't gentle in the ways you see in television shows. She didn't read bedtime stories or talk about feelings. But she was love—pure and unyielding. A mother who risked death to bring lunch to a camp where she didn't even know if her child was. A mother who defied orders just to hold her dying daughter. A mother who swam without knowing how to swim, walked without food, birthed children without rest.

Even now, when she recalls the past, her voice gets soft.

"Po very smart girl," she says. "She save food for me. For Dad. She little, but big heart. She always say, 'Here, Mommy, you eat.' And she not eat enough… She eat leaf… She die because she love too much."

The loss still haunts her. She can't bear to watch war movies. She turns off the television when violence comes on. Some memories live just below the surface, too tender to touch.

But she remembers the small joys, too.

How Vichyini's face lit up when she arrived at the camp that day. How Ratana ran toward her when they finally reunited. How I, a squirming newborn in a sweltering hut, emerged crying and healthy—proof that even hell couldn't stop life.

When she talks about my name, her voice carries a mixture of pride and guilt.

"Panha mean smart," she says. "I want you be smart like your dad. You special boy."

She didn't know I'd struggle with the name later—that in Canada, it would feel foreign, hard to explain. That I'd tuck it away like something to be forgotten. She just wanted to give me strength. A legacy. Something Cambodian.

Her memory isn't what it used to be. Some stories come in fragments. Other times, they flood back in overwhelming clarity, and she has to stop mid-sentence to gather herself.

What she remembers most clearly, though, are her children. Their laughter. Their cries. Their hunger. The way their eyes looked when she saw them for the first time in weeks. The way she could only hug them for a minute before sending them back into the shadows.

And she remembers the escape. The final walk through the jungle. Me in her arms. The world behind them crumbling, and no guarantee of safety ahead.

That's the part that sticks with me—the fierceness. The refusal to break. Not out of pride, but out of love.

She wasn't educated. She didn't write speeches or give interviews. But she built a life from ruins. She raised a family on willpower alone. And she bore witness to one of history's darkest chapters—not from afar, but from the inside.

She still flinches at loud noises. Still worries more than she needs to. Still walks with a limp.

But she smiles when the grandchildren come over. She tells them stories—simpler ones. Softer ones. She cooks the same rice porridge she once scraped together during war, now with plenty of chicken and ginger.

She made it. And nearly all her kids did, too.

That's what she cared about most.

When people ask me where I come from—who I am—I used to talk about my father. His education. His career. His discipline.

But now, I think of her.

Of a girl from a small village who was taught to serve others.

Who lost her childhood, then lost her daughter, then gave everything she had to protect what remained.

A woman who spoke broken English but whose actions spoke perfectly.

A woman who never saw herself as strong but was the strongest of us all.

Chapter 7: He Carried All of Us

John Chhim speaking to other Cambodians, L\location
and date unknown

BEFORE THE KHMER ROUGE, my father lived a life of quiet pride.
He was a factory supervisor in Phnom Penh—a position that gave him
both stability and standing. He had a strong relationship with his
bosses, one a supervisor and the other an inspector, and he spoke of
those days with a clarity and fondness that made it clear: He had

earned their respect. "They trusted me," he told me. "If something broke, they came to me. I could fix anything."

He worked hard and lived well, at least by Cambodian standards of the time. Phnom Penh in the early 1970s, even with the looming threat of civil war, still held pockets of modern life—electricity, steady jobs, and a structured rhythm. My father had a secure job, a home, and a growing family. His position at the factory came with certain privileges: He had a special government-issued card that allowed him to move freely after the citywide 10:00 p.m. curfew, something few citizens were granted. He was proud of this. It meant he was trusted. Useful.

When he described that life, it was with a kind of subdued reverence, as though it belonged to someone else, someone who still had control. He wasn't rich, but he was comfortable. He had responsibilities, friendships, and purpose. His hands—those same hands that would later catch fish in secret to keep us alive—were used to operating machines, not hiding from soldiers.

Then the war came. And everything changed.

On April 17, 1975, the Khmer Rouge rolled into Phnom Penh. Like so many others, my father didn't understand the magnitude of what was happening. Soldiers—young, stone-faced, and dressed in black—marched into the city with megaphones, ordering everyone to evacuate immediately. The city of over two million people emptied in a matter of days. Sick people were pulled from hospital beds. Elderly people, children, mothers carrying newborns—all were forced to leave. My father, like everyone else, had no choice. He gathered our family—my mother and the children—and joined the exodus.

They walked for days. Maybe weeks. He doesn't remember the exact number of kilometers, only that it felt endless. There was no map. No destination. Just the distant hope of reaching somewhere less dangerous. He chose to take our family to his childhood village, a place about fifty kilometers from the capital—familiar ground, at least in theory.

But this return home came at a cost. The Khmer Rouge had no tolerance for people with history. And my father had too much of it.

In the village, word spread quickly. Locals remembered who he was—an educated man with a good city job, a man who had once driven his children to school. To them, that made him suspect. The Khmer Rouge hated professionals. They hated anyone associated with the former government or capitalist systems. They viewed education as a threat. Those who had been literate, respected, or middle class before the revolution were suddenly branded enemies of the state.

My father kept his head down. But it didn't matter. He had already been marked.

And so began the long unraveling.

His mother. His aunt. His grandmother. His cousins. All gone—dead or disappeared in the chaos of resettlement. He never found their graves. He rarely spoke about them again. "They went the other way," he told me vaguely during our interview. "I went this way."

And what lay ahead was no longer a life. It was survival.

In the countryside, the Khmer Rouge split up families based on perceived usefulness. Parents went one way, children another. Men were sent to labor in the rice fields or work camps. Women were assigned to planting, harvesting, or carrying water. My father, stripped of his former title and status, became just another body. A number.

His skills were no longer valued. In fact, they were dangerous. Literacy was enough to get you killed. So he pretended not to know. Pretended not to speak French. Pretended he didn't understand how factories ran. He became another faceless farmer. Quiet. Compliant. Careful.

Still, he watched. He saw everything.

He saw how they starved people on purpose—giving them just enough rice porridge to survive but never enough to grow strong. He saw how they forced people to work from sunrise to nightfall, with no rest, no relief, and no regard for health. He saw how children were turned into spies, trained to report on their own parents.

He learned to fish in secret. At night, while the guards slept or looked the other way, he would sneak to the water with a net—anything he could find to catch what the regime wouldn't give. He knew how to cook the fish so the smell wouldn't travel. Knew how to bury the embers. Knew how to stay alive without being caught. If anyone suspected him, he could have been killed on the spot.

But he didn't get caught.

Instead, he became a ghost. A quiet shadow moving through the fields and trees, always watching, always calculating. "I didn't want to die," he said. "I wanted to live for my family."

There were times he lived alone. Times he stayed with my mother. Times they were separated and only saw each other during rare over-laps in work details. One of the most painful periods was when Po got sick.

After she died, my father changed. He grew quieter. More with-drawn. "That was the worst part," he said softly. "Watching her go."

The regime forced them to continue working even after burying their child—if you could even call it a burial. They never had a proper grave. Today, the place where she was laid to rest is a residential development. There's nothing left to mark her life. Nothing but memory.

But despite his grief, my father focused on staying alive. Out of sight. Out of trouble. He taught himself to survive on nothing. To hide emotion. To expect betrayal. Even kindness became suspect.

And yet, even under those conditions, he remained a man of quiet ingenuity.

When the Khmer Rouge finally fell and Vietnamese forces began to retake the country, he didn't celebrate. He stayed still. Watched. Waited. He had learned that those who reacted too quickly were often punished. "You stay quiet," he told me. "Let others go first. See what happens to them."

Eventually, when the chaos settled, he returned once more to his old village. Not to rebuild—but to prepare for the next chapter. A new kind of escape.

When the Khmer Rouge fell and the Vietnamese took over, most of the country exhaled for the first time in years. But for my father, the war was not over. The scars were deep, the losses permanent. He had survived one regime, but he knew better than to trust the next. In Cambodia, governments changed, but the poor stayed poor, and danger always returned. Freedom was never free. Safety was never guaranteed. And so, he began to plan.

It started with a boat.

He discovered it sunken halfway into the shallows of a riverbank—maybe twenty feet long, wooden, worn from time and tide. It had no motor, no seats, and no owner in sight. To most people, it looked like junk. But to my father, it was the first step toward something else—toward leaving, toward freedom, toward a future beyond the borders of a country that had taken too much.

"I love the water," he told me. "The river was my way out."

He spent days pulling the boat out of the mud, scraping off the rot, testing the seams. It didn't leak. That was enough. He floated it downriver to his village, where he quietly stored it, saying nothing to anyone. Not yet. First, he needed a motor.

That became a mission of its own.

Through a friend, someone he knew from his old life, he found a broken-down military truck abandoned miles away. The engine still worked. The tires were gone, the frame rusted, but the heart of the machine was intact. That was all he needed. Another friend—a mechanic this time—helped him extract the motor, strap it to a cart, and haul it across dirt roads and checkpoints, carefully avoiding attention. They rigged it to the boat.

It wasn't perfect. But it ran.

At this point, most people might have made a run for it. But my father knew better. You don't just flee Cambodia. You escape it slowly, cautiously, pretending all the while that you're not going anywhere. His boat was now a target. People began to take notice. A government-connected man approached him, offered to "test" the boat for "lumber transport." It was a ruse. He was assessing whether it could be used for smuggling—either goods or people.

My father played along.

They loaded the boat with timber and sent it toward Vietnam. He made one trip. Then another. Then a third. Each time, he observed, listened, calculated. He needed money, but more than that, he needed a window—one moment when no one was watching too closely. Finally, on the third trip, the man made an offer: Leave the boat in Vietnam. He would buy it. Pay well. Use it for future transport.

But my father hesitated. Something didn't feel right.

He conferred with another man—a friend he trusted, a quiet ally who had helped him arrange the early trips. This man warned him: Don't leave the boat. "He's not trying to buy it," he said. "He's trying to trap you."

If he left the boat, they could kill him. Strip it down. Take the gold. Arrest or execute him for attempted escape. His friend said the plan was already in motion—someone had been sent to fetch him with a truck, supposedly to "complete the deal." My father didn't wait.

Instead, he left that night.

He took the boat and disappeared into the river.

He brought everything he could carry—my mother, my siblings, whatever food and belongings they could pack. They pushed the boat off the shore under the cover of darkness. There were no lights. Only the sound of water and the whir of the engine, barely muffled under canvas. The current was strong, but he knew the river well. He had fished these waters. Now he was betting his life on them.

They rode through the night, steering through jungle-covered banks and narrow bends. The river was both path and predator—it offered escape, but it could also betray them. Patrols were frequent. One wrong bend, one overheard engine, one flashlight beam—and everything could be lost.

He didn't sleep.

He drove the boat until the edge of exhaustion. When they neared the Vietnam-Cambodia border, he slowed. Hid the vessel among reeds. Waited. There, a new guide—a Vietnamese man with quiet eyes and a calm voice—approached the family. This man was connected, a smuggler of people more than goods. But he had a reputation: He was honest. He agreed to help my father reach Thailand—for a price. Gold.

My father paid. All he had.

Then, with his wife and children, he left the boat behind and continued the rest of the journey on foot.

The path through the jungle was brutal. The forest floor was sharp with roots and stones. Bugs swarmed. Rain fell unpredictably, soaking clothes and slowing movement.

They traveled by night, guided by shadows, hiding from border guards. Vietnamese patrols shot to kill. Refugees were considered deserters—traitors to the regime. The jungle was filled with whispers: families who had been caught, children who had disappeared, bodies found near rivers. But the guide never left them. He led them through the trees, across rivers, and, finally, to the Thai border.

There, my father found a checkpoint. It was not an official crossing, but rather an unofficial handoff point—a place where bribes turned into paperwork and risk into temporary safety. The guide led them to a gate and told my father to walk calmly, say nothing, and board the waiting bus.

He obeyed.

Inside the bus, his entire family sat shoulder to shoulder with strangers—other Cambodians, Vietnamese, Laotians. Some were young. Others were elderly. All had the same eyes—wide, tired, watching for betrayal.

The bus pulled away, and my father never looked back.

They were dropped off at a refugee processing site run by Thai officials and international aid agencies. Here, my father received documents—proof of his status. Not yet free. But now recognized.

What happened next would test his patience even further.

He and the family were relocated to a legal refugee camp. It was crowded, chaotic, and full of trauma. But for the first time in years, he didn't have to hide who he was. He could tell people his name without fear. Could sleep without planning his next move. Could speak without being overheard. Still, the work of freedom was not over.

He began the process of applying for asylum.

He hoped to go to France—his former boss had promised to help. But by the time his application reached Paris, he had already been relocated to a Vietnamese-sponsored refugee site, and the French representative couldn't find him. The opportunity slipped away. "They couldn't take me anymore," he said. "I had already moved."

And so, they waited. Canada accepted them.

In time, they were relocated to Montreal. They arrived with nothing. Not a cent. Not even cigarettes. My father was a smoker, and he remembers those first twenty-four hours in Canada as the hardest—not for the cold, or the language, or the uncertainty—but because he didn't have money for a cigarette and was too proud to ask for one.

"I just sat there," he told me. "Didn't say a word. Just sat there."

He didn't need the cigarette.

What he needed was to rest.

And for the first time in years, he could.

When my father arrived in Montreal, he carried more than just memories of war and survival. He brought with him a deep sense of responsibility—not only to his family, but to the thousands of Cambodians like him who had no roadmap for starting over. He had survived the Khmer Rouge. He had outsmarted betrayal. He had ferried his family across rivers and through forests to safety. And now, he would lead again—not from a factory floor, but from within the growing Cambodian diaspora, building something new out of the ashes.

He didn't wait to be asked. He didn't look for permission. Within months of arriving, he began helping other refugees find their footing —guiding them through paperwork, connecting them with services, helping them understand the bus routes and rental processes and employment forms. He knew what it was like to arrive in a country with nothing. So he made sure others didn't have to figure it all out alone. He helped newcomers understand how things worked in Canada. But he never let them forget who they were. He was Cambodian to his core—proud of his roots, even as he helped others grow new ones.

He wasn't silent. He was vocal, engaged, and respected.

Eventually, he moved the family from Montreal to Windsor, Ontario—looking for better opportunities, more affordable living, and a chance to plant deeper roots. There, he did something remarkable: He founded the first Cambodian Association in Windsor. It became more than just a support network. It was a community. A place where people came not just for help—but for hope.

I remember the gatherings—the potlucks, the music, the speeches. I remember people shaking his hand, smiling when he entered the room. As a child, I didn't fully understand what it meant. But I knew he was important. People treated him like someone who mattered.

He had gone from refugee to community elder. From survivor to pillar.

But leadership didn't mean his life was easy.

To support his family—and to give himself a future beyond survival—he made the bold choice to go back to school. He enrolled in a drafting program to become a professional draftsman. He had always been good with his hands, good with tools, good at solving problems. Now, he would apply that skill in a Canadian context.

The problem was, he didn't have a car.

So he rode a bicycle.

Through the rain. Through the snow. Through freezing winds and long nights. He pedaled across town to sit in classrooms with people half his age, in a language that wasn't his own. And he listened. Studied. Learned. He took it seriously, not just because he needed the diploma, but because he needed to prove, to himself and to us, that nothing would stop him from building a dignified life.

He came home wet some nights. Exhausted others. But never defeated.

I remember once he told us that people laughed at him. "They mock me," he said. "They see this old man riding a bike in the snow and they laugh. But I don't care." He paused, then said something I'll never forget:

"I have to do this, for all of you."

That was his code. His whole life was an act of endurance—not silent suffering, but visible perseverance. He didn't retreat into shame or bitterness. He stood tall. He showed us, day after day, that dignity doesn't come from what you own or how much you speak the language. It comes from how hard you're willing to work for the ones you love.

In time, he earned his diploma.

And he earned respect.

He never stopped talking about Cambodia—but not just the war.

He talked about what it once was. About the life he had before the Khmer Rouge. About the factory he managed. The friendships he built. The dignity he felt when his bosses turned to him for solutions. That life, he often said, was taken from him too soon. But he never let the war define him.

He had a rare kind of resilience—not the quiet kind that hides away, but the defiant kind that rebuilds, organizes, gathers people together and says: "We're still here."

He was a storyteller, too. At family parties, he would sit in the corner and talk—sometimes for hours. His voice would carry over the noise, weaving tales from Cambodia with jokes, warnings, and the occasional life lesson slipped in between. He told stories about jungle crossings, about smuggling boat engines out of scrap trucks, about cooking fish in silence during the war. But also stories about joy— about how proud he was when one of us succeeded, about the food back home, about the time he made something work that shouldn't have.

He wasn't just a survivor. He was a keeper of memory.

Still, there were things he rarely spoke about.

He never mentioned Po by name. Her death was a wound he carried silently. He never blamed the world for what happened. He never wallowed in grief. But you could see it in the way he looked at children—especially the younger ones. There was a softness there, a vulnerability that slipped through the cracks when no one was paying attention.

He worked until his body wouldn't let him.

Even in his later years, he stayed active in the community, checking in on new arrivals, calling people to make sure they had what they needed. He never asked for praise. Never took credit. But those who knew him knew the truth: He helped hundreds of people find their way in a new land—and he did it not out of obligation, but out of empathy.

He understood what it meant to feel lost.

And he made it his mission to ensure others wouldn't have to feel that way alone.

When I think about what kind of man my father was, I think of someone who didn't flinch. Not when the regime came. Not when he was betrayed. Not when he was poor in Montreal or cold on a bicycle in Windsor. He just kept going. Not for glory. Not for recognition. But because he believed in the people he loved.

He never called himself brave.

But he was.

Brave in the way he spoke up for others. Brave in the way he carried his past without letting it break him. Brave in the way he refused to let pain make him small. Brave in the way he laughed. In the way he worked. In the way he loved his family, not with soft words, but with fire and action and relentless forward motion.

That's who my father was.

A man who carried a boat out of a riverbank and turned it into an escape route.

A man who started over in a land that didn't understand him—and made that land a home.

A man who once survived by staying quiet, but later built his legacy by speaking out, gathering others, and building something lasting.

He was not a man who would be broken.

And because of that, neither were we.

Chapter 8: What the Fields Can't Kill

Peter Chhim (author), Thailand refugee camp, date 1979-80

FOR MOST OF MY LIFE, I didn't think I had a story to tell.

I thought the real stories—the ones that mattered—belonged to my parents and older siblings. They were the ones who had lived through the Khmer Rouge, lost a sister, starved in the fields, risked their lives to protect each other. What did I know of any of that?

I was born into the wreckage, yes, but not the fire. That fact alone places me in a strange in-between space. I was technically there. I was a baby in a country being pulled apart by starvation, terror, and forced labor. But I don't remember any of it—not the fear, not the sound of gunshots or the smell of smoke, not the long days of working in the fields like my older siblings endured. My survival was a decision others made for me.

I was the child of aftermath. The one born in the quiet pause between violence and recovery. The one spared by timing, luck, and the sacrifices of others. I've always lived with the weight of what I didn't remember.

It took me a long time to realize that being born after the war didn't mean I was untouched by it. I carried the trauma in a different way—in questions, in silence, in shadows I couldn't name. Only later—much later—did I realize I wasn't alone in that experience. Every second-generation survivor I've met carries some version of that same silence. We inherit the trauma, even if we didn't live it firsthand. We feel it in the atmosphere of our homes, in the expectations we can't name, in the way our parents look at us when we complain about small things.

What I came to understand is that every family carries both visible and invisible burdens. And for second-generation survivors, the burden is often not knowing. We grow up in a strange fog—raised by people shaped by trauma, but never told what the trauma was. We learn not to ask. We learn to read between the lines. And we inherit everything unspoken.

That inheritance shaped me. It made me quiet, reflective, constantly watching the emotional undercurrents in the room. It made me deeply respectful of my elders—sometimes to a fault. It also made me ambitious, driven, and determined to make something of myself—not because I craved success, but because I needed my parents' sacrifices to mean something.

But it also left me with gaps.

Gaps in understanding. Gaps in connection. Gaps in identity.

This book was my way of closing those gaps.

When I sat down to interview Ratha. I wanted to know more about what he remembers, what he lived through. Maybe I was hoping that by hearing his story, I could make better sense of my own. I didn't know if he'd talk. But to my surprise, he did.

And after that, I couldn't stop asking questions.

Each conversation that followed—each sibling, each parent—opened another door. At first, I thought I was doing this just to preserve our family history. But it became more than that. It became a mirror. A confrontation. A long-delayed reconciliation with the weight I'd carried my entire life.

And as I listened to my siblings' stories, something unexpected happened: I began to see myself in them.

Not in the suffering, but in the resilience. The stubbornness. The way they adapted, the way they carried pain without letting it consume them. I started to realize that even though our experiences were different, we shared the same blood. The same drive to keep going, no matter what.

Lori, with her rebellious fire and fierce independence—there were echoes of that in me, especially in my refusal to let silence win.

Ratha, with his protective instincts and emotional distance—those traits showed up in how I navigated my own relationships, even fatherhood.

My father, with his quiet strength and sense of duty—I saw him in how I approach my work, my sense of responsibility, my belief that showing up, day after day, is its own kind of love.

Even my mother, who struggled to speak her story aloud—there's something in that, too. The internalization. The suffering held inside. The way she spoke through action, not words. That, too, became a language I understood.

And in all of them, I saw what I had been looking for: not just their stories, but my place in them. The silence that had once felt like a wall between us began to feel like a space we could finally walk through, together.

I had spent years feeling guilty for being spared. I had felt like an outsider in my own family story. But now I realized: My role wasn't to relive their pain—it was to listen. To understand. To witness. To name the things they had buried for decades.

I'm not a survivor in the traditional sense. I didn't lose a sibling in the war. I didn't labor in the rice fields. I didn't eat grass to stay alive. But I did grow up in the shadow of all of that. I grew up with questions no one wanted to answer. I grew up in a house where grief lingered like dust in the corners.

And now, I am the one who asked why.

Not to interrogate, not to sensationalize—but to understand. To preserve. To hold up the truth so others might see it, too.

That's what *Beneath the Killing Fields* became: a record of survival, yes—but also a reclamation of voice.

Being Cambodian-Canadian has never felt like a clean binary.

I speak English fluently. I grew up in Canadian schools. I play golf. I work in corporate leadership. I've earned advanced degrees. In many ways, I've lived a life of privilege compared to what my family endured. And yet, there is always this other current running beneath it all—this unspoken knowledge that I am shaped by things I cannot fully explain.

I've often wondered: Where do I belong?

In Cambodia, I'm a foreigner. I don't speak Khmer well enough to be fluent in my parents' world. In Canada and the US, I'm often asked where I'm "from." Even now, after decades of living here.

Growing up in Canada, I felt that dissonance constantly. We had made it. We had escaped. But the cost of that escape lived in every quiet dinner, in every look my father gave when a certain memory flickered too close to the surface, in every conversation that ended in a shrug and a muttered, "It's better not to talk about it."

That dissonance used to bother me. It made me feel like an imposter in both places.

But now, I see it differently.

I don't have to choose between worlds. I am the bridge between them.

I carry my parents' history in my bones, even if I don't have the language to explain it all.

I carry my Canadian upbringing in my speech, my posture, my expectations.

I exist in the overlap. And that is not a loss—it's a vantage point.

It's what allowed me to write this book.

I often think about what I'll tell my children when they're curious enough to ask.

They've grown up with access to everything: education, healthcare, freedom of expression. They'll learn about genocides in textbooks. They'll watch documentaries about Cambodia and maybe feel a faint, abstract connection. But unless I tell them—unless I show them—these stories will eventually fade into history.

And I can't let that happen.

Because their bloodline is not just Canadian. It's Cambodian. It's survival. It's endurance. It's sacrifice. And it's also joy, music, community, and love. Our past is not only tragedy. It's culture. It's resistance. It's beauty that refused to die.

I want them to know that.

I want them to know that their grandfather rode a bicycle through snowstorms to get his drafting diploma, because no one would hire him without Canadian credentials.

That their grandmother left behind everything she knew to save her children.

That their aunts and uncles starved in the jungle and still found a way to laugh, to survive, to build a life.

I want them to know that I wrote this book not just for history's sake, but for theirs.

So they would never wonder where they came from.

So they would never mistake silence for absence.

So they would carry the truth forward, even after I'm gone.

There was a time when this history felt like a burden—something heavy I didn't ask for.

But now, I see it as a gift.

It's a painful gift, yes. A complicated one. But it connects me to a lineage of strength, of survival, of story.

This book is for my children, who never knew the Cambodia of my parents but carry its blood in their veins. It's for my siblings, who carried these stories alone for too long. And it's for others—especially second-generation survivors—who are still piecing together the stories they were never told.

And it's for Po.

I never knew her. I never saw her face. I don't even have a photograph of her. Her life is a ghost in my childhood—never mentioned, never mourned in the open, never spoken of until I was in my twenties. And yet, her absence is profound.

There is no grave. No ceremony. The land that may have held her bones is now a residential development. Whatever physical trace of her ever existed is gone.

But she is not gone.

Po lives in every page of this book.

In every silence we broke.

In every tear that finally had permission to fall.

She is the reason I kept going when the writing became difficult. The reason I couldn't allow these stories to fade. The reason I understand, now more than ever, that survival is not the same as healing— and healing requires remembering.

It would be easy for someone to read this book and walk away with a single narrative: that Cambodia is a place of tragedy.

And yes, there is tragedy.

Yes, there was genocide.

Yes, there was starvation, separation, indoctrination, and death.

But Cambodia is also a place of resilience.

It is the sound of monks chanting in the early morning, even after temples were burned.

It is the smell of fried rice and lemongrass in kitchens built from nothing.

It is children learning to laugh again after years of silence.

It is families gathering, dancing, praying, surviving—generation after generation.

I wrote this book not to define Cambodia by its pain but to honor the courage of those who endured it. To show that even beneath the killing fields, life continued to grow.

Because forgetting would dishonor the price that was paid.

Because silence is not the same as peace.

Because remembering is how we break cycles—of trauma, of erasure, of invisibility.

We don't remember to dwell in the past.

We remember to shape the future.

This chapter is the last in the book—but it is not the end of the story.

I don't know what my children will do with these words.

Maybe they'll read them when they're teenagers and roll their eyes.

Maybe they'll return to them in college, searching for identity.

Maybe they'll pass them down to their own children someday.

What I hope, more than anything, is that they will see in these pages a family that refused to disappear. That they will understand that the blood in their veins comes from survivors. That they will feel the strength of a people who endured, who adapted, who rebuilt—not just buildings or homes, but memory, dignity, voice.

And I hope they will keep asking questions.

Even when it's uncomfortable.

Especially then.

Because asking why is not disrespectful.

It is the deepest form of care.

It is how we honor those who came before us.

It is how we become stewards of their truth.

There's a Khmer expression that I carry with me now:

"Karchhucheab ku dauchchea sramol."

"Pain is like shadow."

It never truly leaves us. But it doesn't mean we must live in darkness.

WE CAN ACKNOWLEDGE IT, walk with it, and still find light.

This book is my shadow and my light.

. . .

IT IS the story of a family shattered and sewn back together.

OF A COUNTRY BURIED AND REBORN.

Of a boy born in silence who became the one to ask why.

Not because he had all the answers.

But because he finally understood the value of the question.

Historical Epilogue: Cambodia After the Khmer Rouge

IN 1979, the Khmer Rouge regime collapsed under the weight of Vietnamese military intervention and global condemnation. But for the Cambodian people, the nightmare didn't end when the regime fell. The years that followed were filled with chaos, displacement, and the slow, painful process of rebuilding—not just homes and roads, but memory, trust, and identity.

Pol Pot and other Khmer Rouge leaders retreated to the jungles along the Thai border, where they continued guerrilla warfare for years. For much of the 1980s and 1990s, the country remained unstable. The United Nations didn't even recognize the new Vietnamese-backed government at first; instead, it continued to grant Cambodia's seat to the Khmer Rouge.

Meanwhile, survivors were left to pick up the pieces of their lives in a land filled with ghosts. Mass graves—eventually known as the Killing Fields—were discovered across the country. One former school, Tuol Sleng, had been turned into a torture center where nearly all 20,000 prisoners were interrogated and executed. Today, it is a genocide museum—but even now, many Cambodians cannot bring themselves to visit.

Justice was slow to arrive. Pol Pot died in 1998, never facing a courtroom. It wasn't until the early 2000s that the Extraordinary Chambers in the Courts of Cambodia (ECCC) began trying other senior Khmer Rouge officials. Some were convicted, but many lived out their days quietly, blending back into society.

While the trials brought some closure, many survivors felt they were too little, too late. For most, healing came not through the courts, but through family, storytelling, and spiritual rituals meant to honor the dead.

The legacy of the Khmer Rouge is not just etched into Cambodia's landscape—it is woven into the diaspora. Survivors fled across the globe, carrying their pain, their culture, and their silence. In cities like Long Beach, Paris, Toronto, and Melbourne, entire Cambodian communities rebuilt their lives while wrestling with unspoken grief.

In many families, the genocide was not discussed for decades. Children were raised without understanding why their parents woke screaming in the night, or why they were so protective, or why they rarely said, "I love you." It was only in recent years, through books, interviews, documentaries, and intergenerational conversations, that the silence began to crack.

Cambodia today is a nation of contrast: breathtaking temples, a booming tourist economy, and a young population eager to move forward—but also widespread poverty, political repression, and a deep undercurrent of unresolved trauma. The past lingers in every generation.

This book is one attempt to speak that past aloud. It is not comprehensive. It is not complete. But it is real. These are stories that refused to stay buried.

To the survivors who lived without a voice—

To the children who inherited the silence—

To the ancestors whose names were never recorded—

You are remembered.

You are mourned.

You are not alone.

Acknowledgments

First and foremost, I want to thank my family. This book would not exist without the stories, memories, and emotional labor that each of you shared. To my siblings—Lori, Ratha, Vichyini, and Ratana—thank you for revisiting the darkest corners of your past so that our family's history could finally be preserved. I know how difficult it was to speak aloud what had been buried for so long.

To my mother and father—thank you for your resilience, your sacrifices, and your love. Your courage shaped our survival. Your silence, too, told a story I only now understand. I hope this book honors the journey you endured and the life you rebuilt for us.

To our next generation, and to all the sons, daughters, and grand-children of survivors—may these stories help you understand where you come from and remind you of the strength that flows through your blood.

To my friends and mentors who encouraged me to write, thank you for your belief in the power of memory and story. And to the broader Cambodian community—this book is a tribute to all who lived, all who died, and all who continue to remember.

Author's Note

This book was never meant to be written. For most of my life, the Khmer Rouge era existed in the background of our family story—felt but rarely spoken. The silences were long, the wounds deep, and the trauma often hidden behind quiet routines and distant stares. It wasn't until I began recording interviews with my siblings and parents that I truly grasped the magnitude of what they had survived.

Every chapter in this book is based on real interviews and recollections. Some memories are crystal clear. Others are fragmented, shaped by time and pain. I have done my best to preserve the integrity of each voice while offering historical context where helpful. I've chosen not to fictionalize or dramatize any details. If something seems unbelievable, that's only because the truth often is.

This book is not just about survival. It is about memory, identity, silence, and love. It is about what war does to families and what remembering can do to heal them.

From left to right (Ratana Chhim, Vichinyi Chhim, Ratha Chhim, Sorth
Chhim, John Chhim, Lori Chhim, Steve Chhim, Peter Chhim)

About the Author

 **Peter Chhim** is the son of Cambodian refugees who survived the Khmer Rouge genocide. Born in 1977 while the regime was still in power, he was too young to remember the horrors directly—but grew up in the shadows of their aftermath.

Peter holds a PhD in Industrial & Systems Engineering from Wayne State University and an Executive MBA from Michigan State University. A professional in the fields of quality and process improvement. This book marks his first foray into personal memoir and historical preservation.

Peter grew up in Canada and lives in the United States with his family. He wrote this book to preserve his family's history, honor those who never made it out, and give voice to those who did—so that future generations will never forget.